Toward Fundamental Tax Reform

Toward Fundamental Tax Reform

Edited by
Alan J. Auerbach and Kevin A. Hassett

The AEI Press

Publisher for the American Enterprise Institute
WASHINGTON, D.C.

To order call toll free 1-800-462-6420 or 1-717-794-3800.
For all other inquiries please contact the AEI Press, 1150 Seventeenth Street, N.W.,
Washington, D.C. 20036 or call 1-800-862-5801.

Library of Congress Cataloging-in-Publication Data
    Toward fundamental tax reform / edited by Alan J. Auerbach and Kevin A.
Hassett.
    p. cm.
    Papers presented at a conference held in Washington, D.C.
    Includes bibliographical references and index.
    ISBN 0-8447-4234-1 (alk. paper)
    1. Taxation—United States—Congresses. 2. Value-added tax—United
States—Congresses. I. Auerbach, Alan J. II. Hassett, Kevin A.

    HJ2381.T69 2005
    336.2'00973—dc22

                                                        2005009764

10 09 08 07 06 05   1 2 3 4 5 6 7

In memory of David Bradford,
who led the way toward fundamental tax reform

Contents

Introduction

Alan J. Auerbach and Kevin A. Hassett

To tax and to please, no more than to love and be wise, is not given to men.

—Edmund Burke (1774)

As we write this introduction, President George W. Bush has moved tax reform closer to political center stage than at any time since the Tax Reform Act of 1986. While political forces wax and wane, academic efforts tend to be far steadier. Researchers have spent the period between political debates expanding our knowledge of the possibilities and limitations of tax reform. With the issue on the political back-burner, however, a good portion of this work has yet to meet the public eye.

With this in mind, we invited nine of the leading U.S. tax policy scholars to gather at an informal conference in Washington, D.C. We asked each participant to prepare an article for the meeting that characterized his own views on tax reform. These views—reflecting the latest developments in the academic literature—were to be presented in a manner that would be easily accessible to the general public. This book collects these papers into a single volume.

In addition, although the conversations at the conference were off the record, copious notes were taken of participants' observations during the day. As much of the value of such meetings lies in the identification of areas of consensus and dispute, we have included a final chapter that provides, without attribution, highlights of the discussion, along with a brief overview of the literature that provided the backdrop for the participants' papers.

Why Tax Reform?

As soon as one accepts the self-evident proposition that individual welfare can be improved by government, the necessity of financing government becomes apparent. Conditional on a given level of government spending, the tax-design problem is conceptually simple, at least in its objectives. Government should seek to raise sufficient funds to finance the desired level of spending in a manner that does the least amount of damage possible, while distributing the tax burden equitably.

Damage from a tax can take many different forms. It is generally true that a tax on a specific activity or product discourages the targeted activity or use of the product. If apples are taxed more heavily than oranges, consumers will demand more oranges and fewer apples. If corporate activity is taxed more heavily in this country than elsewhere, activity may migrate away from, or fail to be attracted to, the United States. If the return on savings is taxed, individuals may decide to consume a higher share of their income, and this may reduce investment and growth. Taxes applied to a broad base, with low and reasonably uniform rates, keep distortions low and facilitate administration and compliance. Beyond having a broad base, though, achieving low tax rates typically means reducing the system's progressivity.

This tension between equity and economic efficiency can create a dilemma for those seeking to design an optimal tax system. On the one hand, if every individual faces the same low tax rate, then a highly efficient outcome may be possible. On the other hand, some may view such a distribution of tax burdens as undesirable, since it places the same tax rate on the very poor and the very rich. Differences in informed opinion about the advisability of various tax reforms often emerge because of differing opinions concerning the appropriate weights to place on efficiency and equity.

Although opinions differ in many other dimensions as well, it is a useful simplification to say that the tax-reform community has camps that are divided between two issues. In the first issue, some argue that marginal tax rates should be progressive, increasing along with incomes, while others believe that the equity benefit from significantly graduated rates is not worth the cost in efficiency and, accordingly, advocate a relatively flat rate structure. In the second, some hold that income is the best base for taxation, while others think the base should be consumption. These differing views are fleshed out in detail in the chapters that follow, and the relevant tradeoffs made vividly clear.

If the tax code had evolved over time to some platonic ideal—a broad-based, simple tax with low rates determined by a consensus about the appropriate tradeoff between equity and efficiency—then talk of tax reform would be rare. Against this backdrop, it is productive to take stock of the current state of the tax code. Even a cursory analysis reveals that it is significantly flawed and, conceptually at least, ripe for reform.

Figure 1 provides a handy shorthand description of the income tax in the United States. It plots the marginal tax rate on income for a hypothetical family with two children and two workers for 2004. While a progressive might argue that the rate structure should be upward sloping, and an advocate of a proportional tax might argue that the rate should not rise with income, we are unaware of a coherent philosophical worldview consistent with the crazy quilt of blips that is the current rate structure. Tax experts across the political spectrum concede that such a chart documents a sharp departure from rational policy.

Accordingly, tax reform is widely viewed as desirable, at least hypothetically. As will be clear in the chapters that follow, however, the consensus on this is less impressive than one might suspect. Before one gets too enthusiastic about the wonders that will be accomplished by a sweeping reform, one must understand the forces that produced the grotesque skyline of marginal tax rates in the current code. If powerful political forces will simply move the system back to the current set of rates after reform, then perhaps the reform is not worth the effort. Such an analysis is certainly supported by recent experience. Figure 2 compares the skyline chart for 2004 to the same chart for 1988, just after the last sweeping tax reform of 1986. The relatively simple and elegant code of 1988 presents a striking contrast to the 2004 chart.

This pattern was confirmed more formally in our paper (Auerbach and Hassett 2002), in which we proposed a new measure of horizontal inequality. A broad-based and low-rate structure will invariably treat individuals in similar circumstances similarly. However, a tax code filled with special provisions and loopholes will result in individuals in similar

FIGURE 1

MARGINAL TAX RATES FOR 2004

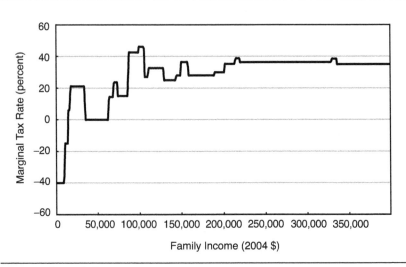

SOURCE: Authors' calculations.

FIGURE 2

MARGINAL TAX RATES FOR 1988 AND 2004

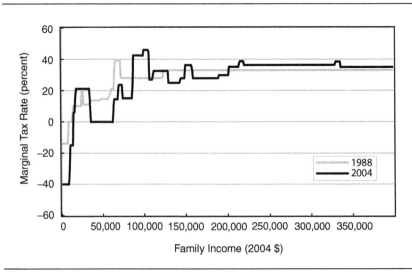

SOURCE: Authors' calculations.

circumstances paying markedly different taxes. That is, the tax code will contain more "horizontal inequality." We found some evidence that the amount of horizontal inequality in the tax code increased after the 1986 reform.

Apparently, much of the base-broadening and tax-rate reduction that was accomplished in 1986 has been lost. Would the same happen again after the next tax reform? What steps might be taken to ensure that it does not?

What Might Reform Achieve?

The debate about the appropriate target for taxation by government dates back many centuries. As early as 1651, Thomas Hobbes argued that government should tax consumption and not wages,

> Which considered, the equality of imposition consisteth rather in the equality of that which is consumed, than of the riches of the persons that consume the same. For what reason is there that he which laboureth much and, sparing the fruits of his labour, consumeth little should be more charged than he that, living idly, getteth little and spendeth all he gets; seeing the one hath no more protection from the Commonwealth than the other? But when the impositions are laid upon those things which men consume, every man payeth equally for what he useth; nor is the Commonwealth defrauded by the luxurious waste of private men.

As will be made evident in the chapters that follow, the distinction between a consumption tax and an income tax is at times quite subtle. However, the chief difference is that an income tax, at least to some extent, taxes the return on savings and investment, whereas a consumption tax does not.

Research concerning the economic effects of a tax reform that moves in the direction of a consumption tax exploded in the 1970s and '80s and has continued to this day. A key early and striking result was provided independently by Kenneth Judd (1985) and Christophe Chamley (1986), who demonstrated that, in the long run, an efficient tax system must not tax capital income.

The intuition of their result is quite straightforward. Recall that an efficient tax system will cause individuals to change their behavior as little as possible. A huge tax on apples and a small tax on oranges would cause an enormous shift away from apples and toward oranges. A small uniform tax on both would not. Think of consumption today as being represented by apples and consumption ten years from now as oranges. If you give up an apple today, you get a number of oranges ten years from now that depends on the interest you got on the money you saved by not eating the apple. At 10 percent interest, a dollar saved today becomes $2.60 ten years from now. If we tax that interest at 50 percent, a dollar saved today only yields $1.63 ten years from now. Clearly, tax on that interest can have a very large effect on how much money you have ten years from now, a very big effect on the rate at which you can trade apples today for oranges tomorrow. Indeed, this distortion grows bigger and bigger over time because of compounding. One dollar saved today produces $17.45 thirty years from now at 10 percent interest. If the interest is taxed at 50 percent, then a dollar saved yields only $4.32 over the same time period. Since it is not efficient for the tax system to create dramatic changes in the relative prices, it cannot be efficient to rely on a device that produces a distortion that worsens steadily over time. This is why a consumption tax has been found to be optimal.

While a consumption tax is therefore more efficient than a comprehensive income tax, according to the analyses of Judd and Chamley, their results rely on assumptions that are quite restrictive. Moreover, even if a consumption tax is more efficient than an income tax, it is not necessarily the case that the efficiency cost of relying on an income tax is high. Numerous researchers have labored to construct economic models of ever-increasing sophistication to allow them to predict the impact on the American economy of a wholesale change to a consumption tax. They have at times found that the gain from a switch to a consumption tax may be enormous. For example, Summers wrote in 1981, "The results suggest that the elimination of capital income taxation would have very substantial economic effects. For example, a complete shift to consumption taxation might raise steady-state output by as much as 18 percent and consumption by 16 percent." These large gains occur because an income tax discourages capital formation, and the increase in capital formation leads to a higher level of economic growth for some length of time.

While these and other results are quite impressive, a number of studies have documented significant uncertainty concerning the exact size of the benefit and credited the gains to other things. The uncertainty arises because modelers need to make assumptions about many behavioral characteristics of firms and workers, and often these assumptions must allow for a wide range of possible behaviors, given existing empirical evidence. A symposium on fundamental tax reform held by the U.S. Congress Joint Committee of Taxation in 1997 provides a useful review of the types of disagreements the literature has produced. A wide variety of models and assumptions was considered by the authors at the symposium. While those that produced the largest effects confirmed Summers's results, others found much smaller effects. The consensus was that, although the impact on the economy of a switch to a consumption tax would be positive, various income-tax reforms might also prove beneficial. For example, the mortgage interest deduction imposes a sharp economic distortion. An income tax that omitted this deduction would be significantly more efficient as well.

Distributional Issues

Even if output and consumption increase in response to a consumption tax, it is possible that tax burdens will shift in a manner that is undesirable from the perspective of distributional equity. Indeed, this view is a primary motivation for many tax-reform design developments. For example, under a value-added tax (VAT)—one pure form of a consumption tax—a firm pays tax on the difference between its total revenue and the cash it has paid to other businesses. Firms are not allowed to deduct wages paid before calculating their tax. Hall and Rabushka (1995) noted that one could reproduce many of the desirable economic benefits of a VAT with a few slight modifications, and allow for the tax to continue serving a redistributive role. Their "flat tax" allows firms to deduct wages before calculating their tax, but workers must pay tax on the wages that they receive at the same rate faced by the corporation. However, workers with low incomes are excluded from the wage tax, a progressive step from a pure VAT.

David Bradford took this logic one step further in the development of his X tax—-which he describes in more detail in his chapter in this volume. He, too, passed the responsibility for paying taxes on wages on to the workers, and then taxed their wages at a number of different rates. In principle, such an approach could allow for any possible level of redistribution, substantially weakening the logical basis of opposition to a consumption tax on social-justice grounds.

Of course, such an approach might throw the baby out with the bathwater. Since graduated tax rates force some citizens to face significantly higher rates than others, and some households to face rates that change considerably over their lifetimes, it might be that a progressive consumption tax relinquishes many of the desirable efficiency characteristics of the consumption tax.

These issues were explored in great detail in a recent paper by Altig et al. (2001). They expanded a model that has been often relied upon in the past to allow them to estimate the impact of tax reform on individuals in twelve different income classes. Some tax reforms, notably the flat tax, increased overall long-run welfare at the expense of the poor, but the X tax was found not only to increase aggregate long-run consumption by 7.5 percent, but also to increase long-run welfare for individuals in every income class. Thus, the latest research suggests it is possible to reproduce the positive benefits of consumption-tax reform in a manner that should be unobjectionable from the redistributive perspective. But the apparent long-run benefits of a carefully crafted system leave very complex transition issues still to be addressed.

Getting There from Here

This brief review reveals why the issue of tax reform demands the attention of so many of our top scholars. The potential gains from reform are, in theory, remarkable. But can such gains be accomplished in the real world? Or are politically popular measures such as the mortgage interest deduction so far off-limits that discussion of such reform will forever be a purely academic affair?

Matters are complicated by the fact that no empirical study exists to date of the long-run performance of a country that has adopted a pure consumption tax as its primary source of revenue. Thus, there is no hard practical experience to draw on to allow us to evaluate competing claims about the economic effect of tax reform. Is the evidence from the models so convincing that it is advisable to take the leap? Can politicians avoid introducing complexity to a new tax system? Can policymakers tax and please?

These and other questions are addressed in the chapters that follow.

References

Altig, David, Alan J. Auerbach, Laurence J. Kotlikoff, Kent A. Smetters, and Jan Walliser. 2001. Simulating Fundamental Tax Reform in the United States. *American Economic Review* 91 (3): 574–95.

Auerbach, Alan J., and Kevin A. Hassett. 2002. A New Measure of Horizontal Inequality. *American Economic Review* 92 (4): 1116–25.

Burke, Edmund. 1774. Speech on American Taxation. House of Commons. April 19.

Chamley, Christophe P. 1986. Optimal Taxation of Capital Income in General Equilibrium with Infinite Lives. *Econometrica* 54 (3): 607–22.

Hall, Robert E., and Alvin Rabushka. 1995. *The Flat Tax.* Stanford, Calif. Hoover Institution Press.

Hobbes, Thomas. 1651. *Leviathan,* chapter 30. http://etext.library.adelaide.edu.au/h/hobbes/thomas/h68l/chapter30.html (accessed March 18, 2005).

Judd, Kenneth L. 1985. Redistributive Taxation in a Simple Perfect Foresight Model. *Journal of Public Economics* 28 (1): 59–83.

Summers, Lawrence H. 1981. Capital Taxation and Accumulation in a Life Cycle Growth Model. *American Economic Review* 71 (4): 533–44.

U.S. Congress. Joint Committee on Taxation. 1997. *Joint Committee on Taxation Tax Modeling Project and 1997 Tax Symposium Papers.* 105th Cong., 1st Sess., November 20. Joint Committee Print. Washington, D.C.: U.S. Government Printing Office. http://www.house.gov/jct/s-21-97.pdf.

1

A Tax System for the Twenty-first Century

David F. Bradford

I. Introduction

When I was invited to contribute this chapter I was asked to organize my thoughts based on a review of my previous work. The gathering of thoughts brings with it a risk of fresh errors. With that risk in mind, I have a variation on past writings to offer in this essay.[1]

In 1976, I experienced a total immersion course in the U.S. income tax system when, in the company of the superb Treasury Department tax policy staff of economists and lawyers, I participated in developing plans to replace it. Our work was in response to a speech by U.S. Treasury Secretary William Simon in December 1975, in which he called the bluff of the tax policy community and ordered the staff to prepare a plan for thoroughgoing reform.

In pursuit of the project, I was for the first time pushed to think deeply about the classic issue of the choice between income and consumption as the basis for taxation. Greatly influenced by William Andrews's *Harvard Law Review* article (1974), which showed how what he called a "consumption-type" personal income tax could solve myriad seemingly intractable problems in the income tax, I became a convert to his point of view. Secretary Simon, however, was unwilling to have us develop a Treasury consumption-tax proposal as the centerpiece of his initiative. Although he was determined to avoid a radical break from

I would like to thank Lily Batchelder for helpful comments.

mainstream reformers like Stanley Surrey, Joseph Pechman, and Richard Goode on the matter of the base, he did agree to allow us to carry along in parallel a consumption-type tax plan.

My guess is that the more conventional approach would have eclipsed the consumption orientation had our Treasury study evolved, as initially planned, into a Treasury proposal for legislative action (as happened in 1984). But President Ford lost his bid for election to a second term, and our work was destined to remain at the earlier stage, where political factors were attenuated. I was gratified that the president agreed to allow the publication of *Blueprints for Basic Tax Reform* (hereafter *Blueprints*; U.S. Department of the Treasury 1977; reissued with some new material as Bradford et al. 1984), which included the two parallel Treasury designs. So it was that two reform plans were set forth in *Blueprints*: the comprehensive income tax (the conventional approach), and the cash-flow tax (a consumption-type tax). The first plan is sometimes credited as the forerunner of the Tax Reform Act of 1986, although neither that plan nor "*Treasury I*," the justly highly regarded Treasury Department study prepared as the basis for the 1986 reform legislation (U.S. Department of the Treasury 1984) picked up *Blueprints*' innovative scheme for integrating corporation and individual taxes. Whatever may have been the merits of the 1986 reform (and I think its lack of durability has to count against its fundamental design), I was disappointed that the choice in 1984–86 had not been for the other fork in the road, toward the cash-flow tax.

The present situation may present another chance to take the consumption fork.

The *Blueprints* cash-flow tax is a purely individual tax; there is no separate tax on companies, corporations, or otherwise. After leaving the Treasury Department, I encountered the Hall-Rabushka (1995) flat tax, which, apart from having an exemption amount for individuals, taxes individuals and businesses separately, but at the same rate. The design, which I call a two-tiered consumption tax (Bradford 1986), seemed to solve a number of problems, and for some time I have refined and promoted a variant that I call the X tax (in addition to Bradford 1986, see Bradford 1987, 1996a, and 1998).

As I explain in this paper, the present inducement to rethink inclines me to put the *Blueprints* cash-flow tax back on the reform agenda, to take over the individual component of the X tax. There are some other fresh thoughts about the X tax as well.

To highlight the promise of the two-tiered consumption tax approach, I present in section II the central design features of the X tax, together with a description of some of the problems in the existing income tax that the proposed system would solve. In section III I sketch why, at a fundamental level, the proposed system is attractive; that is, how, in addition to simplifying and making transparent the tax, it serves traditional objectives of equity and efficiency. In section IV I take up some important qualifications having to do with business tax rate changes over time, especially in the course of transition, and draw the implications for tax design. Section V addresses a similar point in the individual tax. It is at this point that the *Blueprints* cash-flow tax reenters the scene. In section VI, I note a problem in the X-tax treatment of small business and suggest that, here too, the *Blueprints* cash-flow tax offers a possible resolution. Section VII touches on another critical design matter, the treatment of multinational business, and section VIII offers a summing up.

II. The Basic X Tax

Structural Elements. What I'll call here the basic X tax is a variant of the Hall-Rabushka (1995) flat tax. It consists of two components: a business tax and a compensation tax. Under the business tax, all businesses (regardless of legal form) are liable for tax at a single rate. The base consists of the sum of all sales of goods and services (so not including financial assets), including business assets, less the sum of purchases from other businesses (whether on current or capital account). The result is a close relative of a value-added tax, and is sometimes called a "subtraction-method value-added tax." In addition, and unlike the treatment in a value-added tax, payments to workers are immediately deducted.

Individual workers are taxed under the compensation tax, the base of which consists of payments for labor services. (In the basic X tax, if an individual runs a business, it is taxed as such.) Unlike the business tax, the compensation tax is levied at graduated rates, with a zero bracket amount and some set of higher rates on larger amounts received, up to a top rate, which is the same as, or at least no higher than, the business tax rate. In addition, there could be an earned income tax credit, as under the current system.

Important for ease of administration, financial transactions are excluded from both business and compensation tax bases. In the ordinary case, transactions such as borrowing and lending, issue and repurchase of stock, and payment and receipt of dividends do not enter the calculation of the taxable base. (Financial institutions present special problems, which I neglect in this essay. For some details and possible solutions to those problems, see Bradford 1996b.)

The rate of business tax and the rates and brackets of the compensation tax would be set to meet revenue and distributional objectives. I would guess, with a fairly broad conception of the base as far as details of itemized deductions are concerned, we could approximate the progressivity of the U.S. income tax system during recent years with a top compensation tax rate below 30 percent. Having in view the current corporation income tax rate, the business tax rate could potentially be set somewhat higher.

To get a feel for what is involved, note that, if there were no deduction for the payments to workers, the X tax would amount to a single-rate tax on consumption. (I have mentioned the close relationship to a value-added tax.) Economically, it would also be a single-rate tax on earnings, broadly conceived to include the reward for risk taking, entrepreneurship, and invention (since all business income would be taxed at the same rate). Characteristic of this form of tax, the effective rate of tax at the investment margin would be zero, since investment outlays are expensed.

Adding to the system the deduction of payments to workers (where "payment to workers" might include items such as compensation of a person who provided an innovative idea) has the effect of changing the rate of tax to whatever applies at the worker's level of earnings. So for a worker out of the range of the earned income credit but under the tax-free allowance level, the tax—whether thought of as on earnings or on consumption—would be zero.

What Problems Does the X Tax Solve? The X tax makes possible a much simpler and more transparent system than the present one. The most important problems solved by the X tax have to do with what is typically labeled "capital income." I would put at the top of the list of its potential accomplishments removing myriad technical features of the present tax system, features that have little or nothing to do with the fundamental objective of raising revenue fairly. These features also generate substantial compliance costs.

Integrates corporation and individual taxation. Recent years have seen many highly publicized battles in the war to staunch the revenue lost to corporate tax sheltering. A major accomplishment of the X tax is to get rid of a separate tax on corporations. Instead, business (not just corporation) and individual accounts are seamlessly coordinated, a goal long sought by income tax reformers. As a result, for example, complex rules regulating corporate restructuring and distributions, deriving basically from a need to distinguish corporate debt and equity that has never been successfully met in the income tax, would be gone.

Stops wasteful financial innovation. The past couple of decades have seen amazing innovation in finance. A good deal of the ingenuity of Wall Street's rocket scientists is directed toward obtaining the best tax results in connection with any particular economic activity (including making a profit at the expense of the United States and other governments). On the other hand, the tax rules often get in the way of accomplishing new financial arrangements. Both the wasted ingenuity and the obstacle to innovation would be gone in the X tax.

Financial transactions are completely gone from the basic X-tax base of both individuals and companies (apart from the special case of financial institutions). This accounts for enormous simplification.

Resolves the interest deduction mess. The almost incomprehensible web of special rules relating to the treatment of interest payments and receipts that has grown up in the existing income tax would be gone. I regard eliminating the taxation (and deduction) of interest as the essential key to simplification.

Removes capital gains from the tax base. The fights over capital gains would be a thing of the past (business assets are accounted for on a cash-flow basis; individually owned financial instruments do not enter the tax base).

Adjusts the base for inflation. Removal of financial transactions from the tax means that adjusting the base (as opposed to the brackets) for inflation would be feasible, relatively simple, and confined to the business level. (Actually, the adjustment would be completely automatic but for transition considerations to which I allude briefly below.) Correctly regarded as important by tax experts, such indexing is generally considered impractical in the existing system.

Creates a level playing field for investment, including owner-occupied housing. Uniform treatment of business investment would be automatic, regardless of legal entity and rate of inflation, for example, and requiring no judgments about the correct amount of depreciation. (As I shall point out, transition considerations may call for reintroducing some such judgments, but it should still be possible to do much better than under the current system.) Also automatic would be equivalent tax treatment of the yield from owner-occupied housing and business investments. Jorgenson and Yun (2005) conclude that the existing implicit subsidy to owner-occupied housing investment is one of the system's most costly distorting shortcomings. Such neutrality is a practical impossibility under the existing tax system. (I recognize that this virtue of the X tax from the point of view of making the best use of the nation's capital stock may not be among its most politically popular features.)

Cuts the complexity of retirement saving. The immensely complex rules relating to the qualification of retirement saving systems for sheltered treatment would become entirely unnecessary. Essentially, all saving would be treated in a way economically equivalent to qualified retirement plans. So those rules designed to prevent tax abuse (as opposed to fiduciary matters), which are what make this area one of the most specialized in the world of tax practice, would be superfluous.

Facilitates individual filing. A little-noted feature of the X tax is that it would make it easy to use individual filing, thereby eliminating marriage taxes and subsidies. Whether this is desirable as a matter of policy is obviously debatable, but the division of property income that makes individual filing difficult under the present income tax is not a problem for the X tax, since "property income" is taxed uniformly at the business level.

III. Equity and Efficiency of a Consumption-Type Tax

A Reminder of Income and Consumption Tax Fundamentals. As noted, the X tax is a "consumption-type" tax, a term I use to draw attention to the variety of related designs that the approach presents. Students of tax policy are familiar with the distinction between an ideal income tax and an ideal consumption tax at the individual or family level. In the former, the taxpaying unit pays an amount of tax calculated by applying a rate schedule to a base consisting of the sum of the unit's consumption and wealth accumulation during the year (known in the trade as its Haig-Simons income). The *Blueprints* comprehensive income tax made a stab at implementing an ideal income base, but no actual income tax that I know of comes close to doing so. The base of an ideal consumption tax is the same as the base of an ideal income tax except that the wealth accumulation during the year—that is, the unit's saving during the year—is excluded. (Because of the possibility of drawing down savings, consumption can exceed income in a given year.)

The accounting rules needed to put into practice the two forms of tax at the individual level (rather than using company-level methods) are revealing of key differences. (For details, see Bradford 1986 or Bradford et al. 1984.) Conceptually, a person's income is the sum of the change in his wealth between the beginning and end of the year and the amount spent on consumption. The need for a balance sheet valuation (at market value) signals a pervasive problem in income accounting. In practice, we do not actually proceed in this way. Instead, to measure a typical individual worker's income, we proceed indirectly, adding together receipts of wages and salary and various items of "capital income," such as interest and dividends received. The resulting measure will typically fail to match the ideal because of changes in asset and liability values that are not reflected in transaction data. (The theoretical need for the measurement of such asset value changes is the reason we refer to the ideal as "accrual income.")

Basically, because of the failure to account currently for accruing gains and losses on assets and liabilities, the income measure used in practice seriously misses the conceptual target. The consequences are mischievous because of the opportunity the rules present to match financial transactions that are offsetting in their effect on the real economic situation of the taxpayer but lower his taxes. The fundamental tax planning device is to take deductions of interest currently, and to invest in assets that accrue gains that are deferred from tax. Limiting this "tax arbitrage" results in a great deal of tax-rule complexity.

If one were to attempt to implement a tax on consumption at the individual level, the basic measurement strategy would also be indirect. (Again, see Bradford 1986 or Bradford et al. 1984; Andrews 1974 also has an excellent description.) For our typical worker, cash receipts from any source, be it wages, interest, dividends, sale of assets, whatever, would be added together. From this total would be subtracted any amount set aside as savings. The difference has to have been spent on consumption. Only cash transactions are needed. Accruing gains and losses on assets and liabilities have no bearing on the measurement of current consumption.

This basic accounting treatment is readily recognized as that accorded qualified retirement savings in the existing income tax (for example, via an employer-sponsored plan, whereby payments on behalf of a worker are deducted by the company but not taxed to the worker until received in retirement). *If the tax rate is the same at the time of the saving and at the time of subsequent drawing down of savings*, the well-known net effect is to impose no tax on the postponed consumption. The up-front deduction has the effect of producing a government match through the tax system, which is exactly unwound at the time the saving is drawn down for consumption.

If the payoff to saving is unaffected by the tax, the alternative suggests itself of simply ignoring the saving and drawdown transactions. Give no deduction for amounts saved, and exclude from tax any return cash flow. The *Blueprints* cash-flow tax deploys this option, giving individuals wide latitude to choose in which form to save. Amounts deposited to "qualified accounts" (the analogue of qualified retirement accounts) are deducted from the person's base, with subsequent withdrawals included in the base. Alternatively, there is no deduction for amount saved outside of qualified accounts, and return cash flows are ignored. Because there is no deduction, the latter accounting treatment is referred to in *Blueprints* as the "tax prepayment" approach. The tax on future consumption is paid up front, through forgoing the deduction.

Note that, with the tax-prepayment approach, the tax base in any given year *does not* equal the individual's consumption (since amounts saved or dissaved are not counted). With a constant tax rate, the presumption is that, by appropriately adjusting the amount saved, the individual would achieve the same profile of consumption over time, regardless of which form of tax applied.

Both treatments of saving are found in the basic X tax. At the individual level, all financial transactions are ignored. So for the worker, there is no tax on saving. This amounts to the tax-prepayment approach.

At the business level, amounts saved (i.e., invested) are deducted from the tax base. Any amount returned in the future is subject to tax. This is the qualified-accounting approach.

Equity. Suppose one could overcome the accounting obstacles to measuring accrual income. Would there then be any reason to favor consumption over income as the basis for taxation? In particular, does income have the high ground in terms of equity?

To address this issue, it is usual to think of the choice between an income and a consumption base in the context of a person's choice of the timing of working and consuming within a lifetime span. In a system where a single rate of tax applies to either base, the difference between an income tax and a consumption tax is that the latter is neutral in its effect on the timing of consumption, whereas the former makes postponing consumption less attractive. As between two otherwise identical taxpayers (e.g., in the amount and timing of their earnings from work), the income tax puts the heavier burden on the one who prefers to delay consumption until later in life. The consumption tax is also neutral as to the timing of earnings. As between two taxpayers who have the same preferences as to timing of consumption and the same discounted value of earnings, the income tax puts the heavier burden on the one whose earnings come earlier.

Thus, there is a horizontal equity argument in favor of consumption as a base. What about vertical equity? If the horizontal classification of people into classes based on the discounted value of their consumption is accepted as appropriate, presumably the desired degree of progressivity can be attained by appropriate choice of graduated rate schedule.

Efficiency. The efficiency advantage of consumption over income as a tax base is customarily emphasized. The reason is simple: With a consumption tax at a constant rate applicable over time, the person choosing to postpone consumption is rewarded with the full return earned on the invested amount. Under an income tax, by contrast, the saver's payoff is less than the full return by the amount of income tax.

It is well known as a matter of economic theory that this feature of consumption taxation is insufficient per se to establish its clear superiority (Bradford 1980, 1981). Technically, income and consumption taxes are similar in their impact on what is generally considered the most important incentive, the incentive to work (broadly conceived, to include effort and application of talent as well as time employed). Both income and consumption taxes put a burden on work at the margin. As a matter of pure theory, taking into account that the need to raise revenue tends to mean that lowering the rate of tax on one dimension implies raising the rate of tax on another, the superiority of consumption taxation is difficult to establish convincingly.

When one takes into account the virtually inevitable inconsistency of the taxation of different forms of investment that is typical of actual income taxes, by contrast with the potential for consistency under consumption-type taxes, however, my view is that the latter are very likely to be superior.

What if the Tax Rate Is Changing over Time? The discussion so far has concerned a comparison between situations in which a single rate of tax, on income or consumption, applied throughout. Variation in the tax rate over time affects both the equity and efficiency analysis.

To illustrate the implications, suppose the tax rate on an individual changes from 20 percent in one year to 25 percent in the next, where saving is accounted for using the qualified accounting method (so there is measurement of actual consumption). And suppose the change in rate is not anticipated. Now consider two individuals, one of whom had decided to save a lot, and the other of whom had decided to save little and consume a lot in the first year. I have argued that the consumption tax at a constant rate treats these two fairly (technically, the discounted value of their taxes is independent of how they choose to allocate their earnings to consumption over time). With the rate differing between the two periods as in the example, the late consumer is penalized, relative to the early consumer. (A tax rate rising at just the right rate has the effect of imposing an income tax, a fact exploited in Auerbach and Bradford 2004.) If the rate were declining between the two periods, the discrimination would be reversed, favoring the late consumer.

Anticipation of the rate change implies upsetting the efficiency argument as well. Suppose, for example, the going rate of return on saving is 3 percent per year, and consider the options facing the person who contemplates reducing consumption by $1 in the first period. Taking into account the tax saving, reducing consumption by $1 implies putting $1.25 into the qualified account (thereby attracting a tax saving of $0.25 when the tax rate is 20 percent). The 3 percent yield would mean the $1.25 would grow in a year to $1.29. Withdrawing it and paying tax at 20 percent would provide the saver with $1.03 in extra consumption— hence the conclusion that there would effectively be no tax on the yield to saving. But if the tax rate goes to 25 percent in the meantime, the saver would get to keep $0.97 in the second period, as though there were an income tax at a rate of over 100 percent.

The numbers are for illustration only. The key point is that a rate of tax on cash flow that is anticipated to change over time can dramatically affect both the efficiency and the equity properties of the tax. In particular, a rising rate of tax penalizes saving and investment.

IV. Implications of a Changing X-Tax Business Rate

I have noted that, while the *Blueprints* cash-flow tax is a consumption-type tax, it does not attempt literally to measure a person's consumption, year by year. The same can be said of the basic X tax, as a system. In the X tax, saving and investing transactions that would be dealt with on a qualified account basis at the individual level in the *Blueprints* cash-flow tax are shifted to the level of the business firm.

The X-tax business component is based on the firm's cash flow from buying and selling goods and services. A business investment outlay (to purchase a machine, for example) is immediately expensed, attracting the tax saving equal to the tax rate times the amount involved. Ideally, the payoff to the investment should then be subject to the same rate of tax.

A tax rate that varies over time will introduce the investment distortions just described. A natural question is whether one could fix the rate in the law so that this intertemporal variation would not occur. There is one process of change in the tax rate over time that is, however, unavoidable—the transition from a zero rate (before the tax exists) to a possibly permanent positive rate. Even if one could, in principle, imagine a sudden implementation of a new system, the practical reality is that the rule change would be anticipated before going into effect. The more likely phased introduction of a new system would call for attention to the intertemporal tax rate change effects. In particular, I have suggested (1996a) that an easy way to make the transition would be to introduce the X-tax return as a separate schedule on the existing tax returns, with the tax liability in a given year calculated as a weighted average of the liability under current rules and the liability under the X tax.

For example, the transition might be spread over a five-year period, with the tax in year one equal to 80 percent of the bottom line under the currently applicable rules and 20 percent under the X-tax rules. In year two, the weights would be 60 percent and 40 percent. In year five, the weights would be 0 percent and 100 percent; the present system would have disappeared (and could presumably be repealed). Supposing that business X-tax rate is 30 percent, the implication would be an effective rate rising at six percentage points per year.

The problem would be much mitigated if the fact that the effective income-tax rate on companies would be declining as the X-tax rate is rising would have an offsetting effect. It is, however, a little appreciated fact that a changing rate of income tax does not, per se, introduce any special disincentive to invest, provided measured income corresponds to the theoretical ideal (called "economic income" in the tax policy literature). To be sure, actual income measurement falls short of the ideal, but, to a first approximation, all of the impact of the rising effective X-tax rate would fall on investment.

To deal with this problem, I have proposed substituting in the X tax a type of income accounting for business assets (1996a, 1998). Instead of immediately expensing investment outlays, they would be capitalized, along the lines provided for in current rules. (Ideally, the rules would be improved.) As a compensation for giving up immediate expensing, the firm would be allowed a deduction each year equal to an appropriate rate of interest times the undepreciated tax basis in the assets.

Such an accounting approach, if it matched the ideal, would completely neutralize changes in the rate of tax over time. That is, a break-even investment project with one pattern of tax rates over time would remain a break-even project with any other pattern of tax rates over time. The key idea is that the investing firm is compensated for the change in timing of cost recovery (when compared with immediate expensing) by the interest allowance on basis.

The proposed method of dealing with rate changes over time comes, however, at a cost. For one thing, it retains in the tax system the need to identify depreciation schedules for assets, along with related rules applicable to inventories, with their attendant complexity. Perhaps more serious is the need to determine an appropriate rate of interest to allow on basis. Conceptually, the interest rate called for is the one that would make the taxpayer indifferent between expensing and capitalization with interest allowance (in a constant tax-rate environment). But the empirical counterpart is not immediately obvious, risking, on the one hand, economic inefficiency and, on the other hand, political choice of this key tax parameter. Furthermore, capitalization, the carrying of an accounting quantity from one period to the next, implies the theoretical need for inflation adjustment of dollar amounts, thereby losing one of the considerable X-tax advantages, its imperviousness to the rate of inflation.

My suggestion of substituting capital accounting plus interest allowance for the immediate expensing characteristic of the basic X-tax approach was premised not only on a phased introduction of the X-tax rules but also on the idea that one could not reasonably lock in an X-tax business tax rate for the longer run.

Since, however, this essay is an opportunity to rethink past work, I would now recommend choosing a rate of business taxation with the intention to make it stick, perhaps deploying some sort of special majority or other procedural rule, to inhibit change, up or down. I would argue that the compensation component of the X tax provides adequate flexibility to deal with changing economic and political circumstances, the response to which might otherwise be a change in the business tax rate.

The business tax rate should be a fixed point. The fact that the business tax rate puts an upper limit on the compensation tax rate would tend to support erring on the high side in choosing its permanent level. Break-even investments are independent of the fixed tax rate, since the tax relief upon investment write-off balances the tax imposed on future payoffs. The burden on labor supply, broadly conceived, as has been mentioned, to include provision of entrepreneurial effort and ideas, can be dealt with by deducting out payments to the providers of these inputs, to be taxed at the individual level, perhaps at a lower rate.

If this recommendation is adopted, then the capitalization-plus-interest treatment of investment would apply only during the transition period (during which depreciation accounts are needed, in any case, for the residual application of current rules). At the end of the phase-in period, new investment would be expensed, and the then-existing basis could either be expensed or phased out (with interest allowance) over a period of years.

V. Implications of a Compensation Tax Rate Different from One Life-Year to Another

The individual component of the basic X tax, the compensation tax, is calculated using a graduated rate schedule, along the lines of the existing income tax. This means that, even if the rules do not change, in some cases the marginal tax rate will vary from year to year as a worker's earnings vary. Typically, we would expect the worker's marginal (and average) tax rate to be low early in life, high in the middle, and low again in retirement.

This intertemporal variation in the tax rate does not create the mischief that results in the business tax rate, because savings are not included in the compensation tax base. In the language of *Blueprints*, the tax pre-payment approach applies to saving by households. The variation does, however, imply an equity issue: Two workers with the same discounted value of earnings may have different (discounted) tax liabilities.

The issue here is familiar in income-tax policy analysis. A solution that is often discussed and has sometimes been deployed is some form of income averaging. Making a virtue of necessity, *Blueprints* offered individuals an opportunity to self-average, using fairly simple tax planning to choose a mix of qualified and tax prepayment forms of saving. In years of low marginal tax rate, the worker would save in tax-prepaid form, perhaps even supplementing that form of saving with taxable borrowing from a qualified account. In years of high marginal tax rate, the worker would lower taxable income by saving in qualified form, perhaps even using tax-prepaid borrowing to achieve the desired consumption pattern. In this way, the worker could maintain a constant marginal tax rate over the years. (That constant rate would be higher for a worker with higher lifetime earnings, resulting in a tax effectively graduated on the basis of discounted lifetime earnings.)

Although the basic X-tax description does not mention the issue, the distinction between qualified and nonqualified savings is likely to arise as a transition matter. Many people presently have the bulk of their wealth (apart from an owner-occupied home) in tax-sheltered retirement forms. It would make no sense to exclude the drawdown of those savings, which would be subject to tax in the existing income tax, from the X-tax compensation base. They would, appropriately, be treated as deferred compensation (that had been deducted by employers, much as in the X tax). But the result is that workers carrying such savings into the new system would have the same sort of tax planning problem (and opportunity) that we have mentioned for the workers under the *Blueprints* cash-flow tax.

My suggestion, then, is to make the *Blueprints* cash-flow tax the X-tax compensation tax component.

VI. Startups and Small Business

Like the flat tax, the X tax makes a sharp distinction between firms, taxed under the business tax component, and individuals, taxed under the compensation tax component. It is important for economic efficiency that the tax applied to any given firm have a single rate. In the X-tax business component, this is virtually assured, since there is only one rate. There is, however, a potential problem with the treatment of losses. In theory, losses, understood as negative net cash flow, should be compensated by a rebate. This is a problem in the existing income tax as well, but the fact that startup investment is expensed in the X-tax business component means that the problem may more urgently require attention than in the present tax.

The present tax system also offers a potential alternative approach, inasmuch as individual and firm tax accounts are combined for some legal entities (such as partnerships). By careful planning, startup losses of firms can generate savings for owners.

The problem of drawing the line between a firm and the owners of a small business suggests the possibility of deploying similar rules in the X tax. The line-drawing problem in the basic X-tax design would restore to a former prominence the distinction between "earned" and "unearned" income. This unfortunate terminology corresponds to the difference in the X tax between business income (taxed under the business tax) and earnings of workers (taxed under the compensation tax). Where the individual and business tax rates are the same, the classification is of no importance. Arguably, in the flat tax, where the zero-rate segment of the compensation tax is relatively small—so most workers would be at the single rate, which is also the top marginal rate in the compensation tax—cases in which business and compensation tax rates are different would be unimportant. But in the X tax, with its potential for a much more extensive graduation in the individual tax rates, a difference between business and individual rates would be typical.

For a firm with broad ownership, a difference between these two rates might not be a serious problem. But for the closely held firm, a proprietorship, for example, there would be an incentive to pay the worker-owner "too much," in order to obtain the deduction for the firm at the high tax rate, balanced by the inclusion by the worker at the low tax rate. Curbing this practice would call for rules to establish something like an arm's-length level of earnings for the worker. The distinction exists in the present income tax, although it no longer has the prominence it had when there was a maximum tax on "earned income."

The alternative suggests itself of applying to the X tax the *Blueprints* rules for the taxation of business income. In the *Blueprints* system, financial returns at arm's length are subject to the tax-prepaid and qualified-account alternatives that we have discussed. In the case of closely held businesses, however, where the owner's contribution as a worker is difficult to distinguish from the contribution as a provider of capital, *Blueprints* requires that qualified-account treatment be applied. Application of this approach would, to be sure, require a specification of whether the business tax regime applies to any given business firm, but these rules would be grounded in some form of conditions on control, rather than on the purely legal forms that now distinguish standard publicly held C corporations from other business entities. The result would be to address the startup problem in a way rather similar to that used now, and to eliminate the need to distinguish earned from unearned income.

VII. Multinational Business

Given the close relationship between the business tax component of the X tax and a value-added tax, it is tempting to draw the conclusion that the typical VAT treatment of cross-border transactions should apply. The standard VAT is a "destination-basis" tax, which means that exports are not subject to tax, but imports are. The corresponding rule in the X tax would be to exclude export sales from the business tax base, while, by denying a deduction for them, import purchases are in effect subjected to tax.

I have written at some length on this issue (2004). The theoretical argument is compelling that, apart from transition effects, there is no economic difference between the destination-basis approach and the alternative "origin-basis" approach, whereby export and import sales and purchases by the firm are treated like any other (as in the present income tax). Nevertheless, there is little doubt that the "border adjustment" of export and import transactions would have enormous political appeal. The idea that it would be good for U.S. business may be the main source of support for a VAT or equivalent tax.

A destination-basis tax would solve, at a stroke, a persistent dilemma in international taxation: the transfer-pricing problem, which would exist in amplified form in an origin-basis X tax. In doing business with its foreign subsidiaries, a U.S. multinational corporation has the potential to set the terms of transactions artificially (for example, the prices charged a subsidiary for parts produced in the United States) to influence the location of profits, typically to shift them abroad where relatively favorable treatment may be given. In the existing income tax, the problem is somewhat mitigated by the fact that what is involved is deferral of U.S. taxation. Profits repatriated in the form of dividends from subsidiary to parent are subject to U.S. tax. In the X-tax context, where financial transactions are eliminated from the base, the potential is for complete avoidance of tax.

With a destination-basis approach, the terms of export and import transactions, whether within a multinational family of companies or at arm's length, are of no importance, since export sales would be excluded from the U.S. company's X-tax base, and import purchases are not deductible.

Unfortunately, the destination-basis approach has the disadvantage that changes in the tax rate affect the equilibrium relationship between the domestic and foreign price levels or the equilibrium international exchange rate. Suppose, to take an example, with the present income tax rules, the exchange rate is $1 to EUR 0.80. Neglecting transportation costs, an item that sells for EUR 1 in Paris will be expected to sell for $1.25 in New York. With present rules, the importer pays $1.25 for the EUR 1 needed to buy the item in France, and breaks even on the sale in New York, since the purchase amount is deducted from the sales proceeds in determining the U.S. tax. Suppose the rules are changed to a destination basis, and the U.S. business tax rate is 30 percent. Now there is no deduction for the imported item. If the exchange rate is fixed, the importer has to sell the item for $1.79 ($1.79 less 30 percent is $1.25, which is what the importer has to pay for it). We can fix the picture by changing the general price level in the United States, by lowering the price level in Europe, or by changing the exchange rate, from $1 to EUR 0.80, to $1 to EUR 1.14. The change in tax treatment amounts to a 30 percent increase in the rate applied to imports; to compensate for it requires a 30 percent strengthening in the dollar in the international exchange market.

As in the case of the transition to cash-flow accounting in the purely domestic context, the impact of the change in the tax rate in the international setting has equity and efficiency effects. These effects would, furthermore, be repeated whenever there is a change in the business tax rate.

In my previous work on this problem, I have concluded it would probably be preferable to avoid these stresses. I proposed possible rules that might preserve the origin-basis character of the U.S. tax system but still deal reasonably effectively with the transfer-pricing problem in taxing multinational firms. This is not the place to attempt to summarize the proposed design, which is far from having been rigorously tested. Rather I would observe that, if it is possible to put in place a business tax rate that can be expected to be highly stable, it may well be worth looking for ways to ease the effects I have mentioned of a rising rate of X tax, so as to make a once-and-for-all transition to a destination-basis tax, with its considerable administrative advantages.[2]

VIII. Summing Up

In this essay I have sketched and attempted to justify the X tax as a replacement for the present income tax on individuals and corporations.

The basic X tax comprises a two-part system. The *business tax* is paid at a single rate by businesses of all forms. The business tax base consists of all sales by the business less all purchases from other businesses, and less payments to workers (including amounts set aside for pensions). Individuals pay *compensation tax* only on the payments for work, including receipts from pensions.

Here I have suggested the following refinements of this basic design:

- Use a system of capitalization of business investment plus interest allowance on business asset basis during a transition period.

- Emphasize the need for a highly stable rate of business tax. When it is reached in a phased transition, go to full expensing of new business investment and phase out the basis-plus-interest allowance residual over time.

- Use the *Blueprints* cash-flow tax as the individual component of the X tax. In particular, permit individuals to self-average the tax through the use of tax-prepayment and qualified-account forms of saving.

- Extend the *Blueprints* cash-flow tax application to closely held businesses, taking them out of the separate business tax, which would apply to businesses that are not closely held.

- Consider using a destination basis for international business transactions, whereby export sales are excluded from the base and no deduction is allowed for import purchases. The highly stable business tax rate is critical in this context. Finding ways to mitigate the impact of the economic effects of a transition to the destination-basis system would merit careful attention.

As I indicated in the introduction, there are risks in trying out new ideas. I hope the upside prevails.

Notes

1. I have included most of those writings in the reference list, in particular, Bradford (1986, 1987, 1996a, 1996b, 1998, 2000 [a collection of many of my papers on taxation], 2001, 2004); Bradford and Slemrod (1996); and Bradford et al. (1984).

2. Imports and exports by small businesses should be dealt with in a separate schedule, at the "big business" tax rate.

References

Andrews, William D. 1974. A Consumption-Type or Cash Flow Personal Income Tax. *Harvard Law Review* 87 (April): 1113–88.

Auerbach, Alan J., and David F. Bradford. 2004. Generalized Cash-Flow Taxation. *Journal of Public Economics* 88, no. 5 (April): 957–80.

Bradford, David F. 1980. The Case for a Personal Consumption Tax. In Joseph A. Pechman, ed. *What Should Be Taxed: Income or Consumption?* 75–125. Washington, D.C.: Brookings Institution Press.

———. 1981. Issues in the Design of Savings and Investment Incentives. In Charles R. Hulten, ed. *Depreciation, Inflation and the Taxation of Income from Capital*, 13–47. Washington, D.C.: Urban Institute.

———. 1986. *Untangling the Income Tax.* Cambridge, Mass.: Harvard University Press.

———. 1987. On the Incidence of Consumption Taxes. In Charles E. Walker and Mark A. Bloomfield, eds. *The Consumption Tax: A Better Alternative,* 243–61. Cambridge, Mass.: Ballinger. Revised version published as Bradford, David F. 1988. What Are Consumption Taxes and Who Bears Them? *Tax Notes* 39, no. 3 (April 18): 383–91.

———. 1996a. *Fundamental Issues in Consumption Taxation.* Washington, D.C.: AEI Press. Expanded version of Bradford, David F. 1996. Consumption Taxes: Some Fundamental Transition Issues. In Michael J. Boskin, ed. *Frontiers of Tax Reform*, 123–50. Stanford, Calif.: Hoover Institution Press.

———. 1996b. Treatment of Financial Services under Income and Consumption Taxes. In Henry J. Aaron and William G. Gale, eds. *Economic Effects of Fundamental Tax Reform,* 437–64. Washington, D.C.: Brookings Institution Press.

———. 1998. Transition to and Tax Rate Flexibility in a Cash-Flow Type Tax. In James Poterba, ed. *Tax Policy and the Economy.* Vol. 12, pp. 151–72. Cambridge, Mass.: MIT Press.

———. 2000. *Taxation, Wealth, and Saving.* Cambridge, Mass.: MIT Press.

———. 2001. Blueprint for International Tax Reform. *Brooklyn Journal of International Law* 26, no. 4:1449–63.

———. 2004. *The X Tax in the World Economy: Going Global with a Simple, Progressive Tax.* Washington, D.C.: AEI Press.

Bradford, David F., and Joel Slemrod. 1996. *Making Tax Choices.* Washington, D.C.: Nathan Associates, Inc.

Bradford, David F., and the U.S. Treasury tax policy staff. 1984. *Blueprints for Basic Tax Reform*, 2nd ed. Washington, D.C.: Tax Analysts. Originally published as U.S. Department of the Treasury (1977).

Hall, Robert E., and Alvin Rabushka. 1995. *The Flat Tax.* 2nd ed. Stanford, Calif.: Hoover Institution Press.

Institute for Fiscal Studies. 1978. *The Structure and Reform of Direct Taxation: The Report of a Committee Chaired by Professor J. E. Meade*. London: George Allen & Unwin.

Jorgenson, Dale, and Kun-Young Yun. 2005. Efficient Taxation of Income. In T. J. Kehoe, T. N. Srinivasan, and J. Whalley, eds. *Frontiers in Applied General Equilibrium Modeling*, 173–218. Cambridge: Cambridge University Press.

U.S. Department of the Treasury. 1977. *Blueprints for Basic Tax Reform*. Washington, D.C.: U.S. Government Printing Office. January. Reissued as Bradford et al. (1984).

———. 1984. *Tax Reform for Fairness, Simplicity, and Economic Growth*. Vols. 1–3. Washington, D.C.: U.S. Government Printing Office. November.

2

Tax Reform Options in the Real World

William G. Gale

Introduction

The basic description of a desirable tax system is broadly accepted: It should raise the revenues needed to finance government spending in a manner that is as simple, equitable, stable, and conducive to economic growth as possible. Although people agree that the current system clearly falls short of at least some of these goals, it is not easy to point to examples around the world that work much better. In addition, how the system should be reformed is subject to enormous controversy. People define the underlying goals differently—notions of fairness, for example, are clearly "in the eyes of the beholder." People disagree on the most effective policies for attaining a particular goal, such as more economic growth. And most importantly, people have differing value judgments, which make agreement on policy almost impossible in the nearly ubiquitous case where there are tradeoffs among the goals.

In addition, although all of us are attracted to well-designed tax reforms, the real challenge is changing the system in a way that will work not only on paper but also in the real world. In practice, the changes needed to make idealistic tax proposals acceptable in a world populated by politicians, lobbyists, tax shelter experts, and taxpayers who want their own individual taxes cut and who have strong but malleable views on equity and enforcement almost always make taxes more complex, less fair, and less consistent with economic prosperity. Nevertheless, there is currently a real opportunity for tax reform that should be taken seriously.

Driving Forces for Reform

In addition to ongoing concerns about the complexity, inequity, and inefficiency of the current system, at least three factors imply a pressing need for significant changes to the tax system.

First, the central tax question facing the country currently is not tax reform, but the extent to which the Bush administration's tax cuts—all of which expire between now and 2010—should be made permanent and, if so, how they would be financed. The loss in revenues from making the tax cuts permanent would be enormous: equal to several times the resources needed to repair the entire Social Security problem, which the president has declared a "crisis" (Gale and Orszag 2004a). We do not know how this fiscal hole would be filled because, despite advocating basically the same tax policy since 1999, the administration has never proposed a way to pay for the cuts and, in each of the last two years, actually proposed to change the accounting rules in a way that would have let the tax cuts be made permanent without even showing a cost in the budget baseline. In fact, the tax cuts can only be paid for with increases in other taxes or lower spending. The required changes, though, would be enormous. For example, in 2015, if reductions for Social Security, Medicare, Medicaid, defense, homeland security, and net interest were off limits, the rest of federal spending would have to be cut by almost half, just to pay for the revenue loss from the tax cuts. Alternatively, a roughly 120 percent increase in corporate tax revenues would cover the revenue loss. To the extent that tax increases or spending cuts do not occur soon—and they do not seem likely—the revenue losses would have to be financed by borrowing, which merely postpones the ultimate payment. Moreover, the net effect of the tax cuts plus borrowing would be to reduce long-term economic growth, according to studies by academics and the Congressional Budget Office (Gale and Orszag 2004b), which would put the nation in a weaker long-term economic situation.

The second problem is the alternative minimum tax (AMT). Taxpayers pay the AMT when their AMT liability exceeds their regular income tax liability. Designed in the late 1960s and strengthened in 1986, the AMT operates parallel to the regular tax system and was originally intended to capture tax on excessive sheltering activity. The tax has evolved, however, so that it does not tax many shelters and it does tax a variety of items—like having children, being married, or paying state taxes—that most people do not consider shelters. Moreover, the number of taxpayers facing the AMT is slated to grow exponentially, from about 3 million today to 30 million by 2010, under current law, both because regular taxes are slated to fall and because the AMT is not indexed for inflation. This expansion will increase the inequity and complexity of the tax system (Burman, Gale, and Rohaly 2003).

The third issue is the expected increase in government spending over the next several decades. Since 1950, tax revenues have hovered between 16 and 20 percent of gross domestic product (GDP). Under current projections, however, government spending is expected to rise to about 27 percent of GDP by 2030 (Rivlin and Sawhill 2005). This increase is fueled mainly by rising entitlement spending for Social Security and especially Medicare and Medicaid, trends which are fueled in turn by increases in the number of elderly households and in health-care expenditures per capita. Unless the country is willing to make truly massive cuts in such expenditures relative to their projected values, a significant increase in revenues above 20 percent of GDP will be required. Federal revenues in 2004 were at their lowest share of GDP since 1959. If the tax cuts are made permanent and the AMT reduced to manageable levels, revenues would be a smaller share of GDP when the baby boomers begin retiring en masse in about five to seven years than the average revenue share over the past thirty years. This would leave the country unprepared for addressing the coming budget problems.

All of these issues will play out against the backdrop of a political system that features both houses of Congress and the White House held by a majority party whose members have overwhelmingly signed the "no new taxes" pledge, yet who also voted overwhelmingly for the largest entitlement increase in recent history (the Medicare prescription drug benefit), cut taxes four times in four years (Gale and Kelly 2004), and in 2004 passed one of the most loophole-laden tax acts in recent memory.

Fundamental Reform

The most radical approach to tax reform would be to junk the whole system and start over. Under a national retail sales tax (NRST), for example, a single tax rate would apply to all sales by businesses to households.

Sales between business and between households would be untaxed. Under a value-added tax (VAT), each business would pay tax on the sum of its total sales to consumers and to other businesses, less its purchases from other businesses, including investments. Thus, the increment in value of a product at each stage of production would be subject to tax. Cumulated over all stages of production, the tax base just equals the value of final sales by businesses to consumers—that is, the same in theory as in an NRST. The flat tax, originally developed by Hoover Institution scholars Robert Hall and Alvin Rabushka (1995), is simply a two-part VAT: The business tax base would be exactly like the VAT except that businesses would also be allowed deductions for wage payments and pension contributions. Individuals would pay tax on wages and pension income that exceeded personal and dependent exemptions. Businesses and individuals would be taxed at a single positive flat rate.

The NRST, the VAT, and the flat tax are all flat-rate, broad-based consumption taxes. Advocates claim that fundamental tax reform could boost growth significantly, slash tax burdens, simplify compliance, and eliminate the IRS. Unfortunately, however, a more realistic assessment is less sanguine.

The required tax rate in the national retail sales tax to replace almost all existing federal taxes and maintain government programs would be at least 40 percent and probably significantly higher—not the 23 percent rate advertised by its supporters (Gale 1999).

The pure flat tax could replace the existing income and corporate tax with a rate of about 21 percent if there were no serious avoidance problems (but see below). But doing so would cause significant relocation in the economy, and declines in charitable contributions, real housing prices, and the number of households with health insurance (Aaron and Gale 1996). Businesses' tax liability would vary dramatically relative to the current system, and they would find taxes were no longer based on profits (Hall and Rabushka 1995). Realistic versions of the flat tax—which smoothed out these problems by allowing transition relief; individual deductions for mortgage interest, charity, and state taxes; and business deductions for health insurance and taxes—would require tax rates of 30 percent or higher (Aaron and Gale 1996).

These rate estimates assume there is little or no (legal) avoidance or (illegal) evasion of taxes. But experience in other countries shows that a national retail sales tax would have difficulty controlling tax evasion if rates went much above 10 percent. Under the flat tax or X tax, a variant of the flat tax that would introduce graduated taxation of wages, firms could easily relabel cash flows and reduce their taxes substantially (McLure and Zodrow 1996).

Both the NRST and the flat tax would provide large tax cuts for the wealthiest households and make up the revenue with tax increases on low- and middle-income households. The X tax has the potential to be somewhat more progressive than the flat tax.

Many of the problems and tradeoffs created by fundamental tax reform could be mitigated if reform boosted growth dramatically. In their pure form, the NRST, flat tax, or X tax could have positive effects on economic growth, but when the taxes were subjected to the realistic considerations noted above and the higher tax rates such considerations would require, studies suggest that the taxes would likely generate little if any net growth and could actually reduce growth (Aaron, Gale, and Sly 1999; Altig et al. 2001).

An alternative fundamental reform plan, the USA tax, would replace the existing tax system with a VAT on businesses with a personal consumption tax. Under the personal tax, people would report all income from earnings, investments, and receipt of loans, but they would be allowed a new deduction for all net saving and repayment of loans. Thus, the personal tax falls on the difference between income and saving, which is consumption. In addition, the USA tax would retain some of the deductions and credits allowed under the current personal income tax and would have progressive rates. The USA tax has been judged to have substantial administrative problems.

Five Easy Pieces

Completely replacing the existing system would create significant administrative, legislative, and economic upheavals. This has led some to advocate piecemeal or partial replacement of the income tax system.

The basic notion is that by making changes one at a time, progressive taxes on income and wealth can be transformed into a flat consumption tax. The changes typically include: reductions in marginal income-tax rates, especially for high-income households; increases in contribution limits for tax-preferred savings accounts; expensing (immediate write-offs) of business investment, rather than depreciation over time; repeal of the estate tax; and a reduction in dividends and capital gains taxes. Many of these items are reflected in the administration's recent rate cuts, dividend and capital gains tax cuts, expansions of contribution limits to IRAs and 401(k)s, and temporary "bonus depreciation" provisions. The administration has also promoted expanded tax-free savings accounts.

The problem is that these changes do not add up to a well-defined tax system. A well-designed consumption tax would (a) collect adequate revenues to cover expenditures over time and avoid reducing national saving through higher government deficits; (b) broaden the base to lessen interference in the economy; (c) tax already-existing capital—that is, concentrate any revenue relief on new saving or investment; and (d) treat interest income and expense in a consistent manner. But the recent changes and the piecemeal proposals fail all four tests. In combination, they (a) lose substantial amounts of revenue; (b) do not broaden the base; (c) reduce taxes on existing capital; and (d) increase the difference in the tax treatment of interest income and expense.

Some tax overhaulers downplay such concerns, arguing that the criticisms represent the perfect being the enemy of the good. But the underlying point is that the system that emerges has many of the worst features of *both* the previously existing tax system and a fundamentally reformed system. First, the tax cuts accompanied expenditure expansion, leading to deficits that may reduce long-term economic growth. Second, there will be no efficiency gains from broadening the base if no base-broadening occurs. Third, there will be efficiency losses from increasing taxpayers' ability to shelter income if there are enlarged differences between the taxation of capital income and capital expense. Particularly important here is the tax treatment of interest payments. A well-designed income tax would tax interest income and allow deductions for interest payments. A well-designed consumption tax could tax borrowing and allow deductions for lending (saving), or it could allow for nontaxation of interest income *coupled with nondeductibility of interest payments.*

The key point is that *any* well-designed tax system would treat capital income and capital expenses in a symmetric, consistent manner. Proposals for expanded tax-preferred saving accounts would move the system even further toward treating the two sides of the ledger inconsistently and increase opportunities for tax sheltering.

Finally, since it seems likely that high-income households are more financially sophisticated and can better afford financial advice, proposals simply to expand nontaxable saving deposit vehicles could lead not just toward a wage tax, but toward a wage tax that was paid only by low- and moderate-income households (who could not so easily reduce their tax base even below wages paid through the use of interest deductions).

"Back to the Future"

Yale University Law Professor Michael Graetz has a proposal he describes as "Back to the Future" (Graetz 2004). He would, among other things, raise the income tax exemption to about $100,000, tax income above that level at a flat 25 percent tax rate, remove some shelters from the income tax, and cut the corporate tax rate in half. This would cut revenues from these taxes in half, and the lost revenue would be replaced by a broad-based VAT.

This proposal has significant advantages. It would reduce the number of income tax returns filed by roughly 100 million. Transition problems would be reduced relative to fundamental reform because the income tax and corporate tax would not be abolished.

But there are also a number of concerns. The main issue is that the proposal has not been specified in sufficiently detailed manner to gauge its effects. Relevant details include what would be excluded from the VAT base; which low-income credits would be retained, and what mechanism would be used to provide those credits (since these households would not file income tax returns); and how the income tax base would be structured. Although the proposal is intended to be neutral with respect to revenue and distribution, in the absence of additional details it is unclear what the implications of those constraints are for the required tax rates and relevant tax bases. My own estimates suggest that a VAT rate of about

15–20 percent would be required, which would make it difficult to maintain distributional neutrality. Also, if states did not abolish their income tax or raise their exemptions to $100,000, there would be little saving in tax complexity.

Real-World Reforms

The following options may be less ambitious than the ones discussed above, but may in turn prove more enactable and indicate ways that the existing system could be made simpler, fairer, more conducive to economic growth, and consistent with spending needs.

Integrate the Corporate and Individual Income Taxes. Only about a quarter of corporate income appears to be taxed at both the individual and corporate level, and all of that is now taxed at a maximum rate of 15 percent at the personal level. Corporate income can avoid taxes at the corporate level through shelters. It can avoid taxation at the individual level to the extent that it accrues to nonprofits and pensions. About one quarter of corporate income is taxed at the individual level, but not the corporate level; one quarter is taxed at the corporate level, but not the individual level; and one quarter appears never to be taxed (Gale and Orszag 2003). While the emphasis and public discussion have been on the so-called double taxation of corporate income, the nontaxation of corporate income is probably an even bigger problem.

Reforming, or integrating, the individual income tax and corporate income tax should involve several features that need to be dealt with *simultaneously*. First, the integration should occur only for income stemming from *new* corporate investment. There is no reason to give tax breaks on the income stemming from old investments; those tax breaks would be windfall gains. Second, individual-level taxation of corporate dividends and capital gains (on new investments) should be removed only if the full tax has been paid on the income at the corporate level. If corporate taxes were not paid, then corporate dividends and capital gains should be taxed at the *full* individual rate (not capped at 15 percent). Third, efforts to shut down corporate tax sheltering need to be beefed up substantially. This could include increased enforcement as well as altered accounting procedures that require more conformity between book and taxable income. Fourth, a wholesale attack on corporate tax expenditures would be a final, key element in this package. To be clear, my sense is that this package of changes would likely raise net federal revenues from corporate source income.

Integrate the Payroll and Individual Income Taxes. For about 70 percent of all households, and virtually all filers in the bottom 40 percent of the income distribution, payroll tax burdens exceed income tax payments (Tax Policy Center 2003). The payroll tax imposes a burden of roughly 15 percent on the very first dollar of earnings. In contrast, a family of four with all of its income from wages does not fall into the 15 percent marginal income tax bracket until its income exceeds $36,000, and it does not pay an average 15 percent income tax rate until its income is $120,000, which is actually higher than the payroll tax cap for Social Security. Integrating the payroll tax and the income tax could take different forms, but each would make the burden of payroll taxes more progressive. This would be particularly important if a consumption tax either were added to the system or replaced part of the system, to offset some of the regressivity of that tax.

Simplify. There are a number of ways to simplify the system, even without enacting fundamental reform. The administration's efforts to unify the definition of a child in the tax code are one such example. Return-free filing could be achieved for as many as 50 million taxpayers with relatively minor changes in the tax code (Gale and Holtzblatt 1997). Return-free filing is in existence in dozens of countries around the world and would relieve the hassles of filing and compliance for the households least able to address such issues. The number of households who could avoid filing would be greatly enhanced, and other simplifications would occur, if the personal exemption, the child credit, and the earned income credit were consolidated into a single program, and if the standard deduction were increased. Likewise, increasing the standard deduction by the value of a personal exemption and reducing the number of personal exemptions by one would simplify taxes further by reducing the number of people who itemize. In addition, education subsidies could be consolidated and streamlined, as could retirement saving programs.

Restructure Deductions into Credits. On simplicity, equity, revenue, and possibly efficiency grounds, the itemized deductions should be converted to refundable, flat-rate, capped credit. Although they are immensely popular and subsidize activities thought of as "good," itemized deductions create numerous problems. They largely subsidize activity that would have occurred anyway. They complicate tax filing and enforcement. They erode the tax base and are regressive, giving bigger benefits to high-income than low-income filers. Finally, the deductions hide subsidies that would be obvious if they were spending programs. Imagine that instead of a mortgage interest deduction, we had a program called "homeowner welfare," in which taxpayers earned a "welfare entitlement" equal to their annual mortgage interest payment times their tax rate. Anyone whose entitlement was below a certain threshold, say $6,000, would receive nothing. Anyone whose entitlement exceeded the threshold would receive the entitlement in cash. This program would be decried as wasteful and a sop to the rich. Yet it is not dissimilar to the way the mortgage interest deduction works. Items that represent true reductions in ability to pay taxes should be deducted in full, but none of the itemized deductions completely meets that standard. Relative to current law, converting the deductions to 15 percent credits would reduce revenue loss, dampen regressivity, minimize the other unfair aspects of deductions, and simplify tax filing. At the same time, it would continue to allow a subsidy for activities that society may deem as "preferred" for one reason or another.

Fix the Alternative Minimum Tax. The alternative minimum tax should be abolished, if—and these are some big ifs—(a) the anti-tax-sheltering provisions of the AMT are brought into the income tax, (b) dividends and capital gains are taxed as described above, and (c) the revenue is made up by adjusting income tax rates. Alternatively, the AMT could be retained, but reformed in a revenue-neutral manner that would raise the AMT exemption substantially, to remove the middle class from the tax, and would include dividend and capital gains as preference items, to restore the AMT's goal of closing shelters.

Raise Private and National Saving. The enormous efforts over the past twenty-five years to stimulate private saving by providing tax incentives for *contributions* to particular accounts (which is quite different from "saving") do not appear to have been very successful in raising overall private saving, and they have been even less successful in raising national saving, the sum of private and public saving. Currently, federal tax expenditures for pensions and other saving incentives are larger than the entire level of personal saving (Bell, Carasso, and Steuerle 2005).

Part of the problem is that the accounts do not subsidize saving, which requires a reduction in consumption spending and living standards. Instead, they merely subsidize contributions into an account. These contributions can be made in many "painless" ways that do not involve reducing one's living standard. High-income, high-wealth households are the most able to make such painless contributions, drawing from income they would have saved anyway or assets they already have saved. Another part of the problem is that the immediate incentive to contribute—as measured by the tax deductions that are allowed—is largest for the same high-income households. Finally, the ability to finance the contributions to such accounts with debt on which interest payments are deductible creates tax shelter opportunities and should be restricted, as the chapters in this volume by Hall, Pearlman, and Slemrod point out.

Studies that acknowledge the role of precautionary needs for saving and the extent of saving incentives already in the current system generally find that a consumption tax would have a very small impact on the national saving rate (Engen and Gale 1996). In short, if increasing saving is the problem, tax reform is unlikely to be the answer.

A much more effective, less expensive, and simple approach to encouraging national saving—and the economic growth it can generate—is to improve the operation of existing accounts by encouraging automatic enrollment and automatic escalation of contributions over time in existing 401(k) accounts. This would raise contribution rates among low- and moderate-income workers, who are less likely to be using the accounts as tax shelters. Likewise, encouraging people to save their tax refunds or allowing automatic payroll deductions for individual retirement accounts would have similar effects. Relative to increasing contribution limits for tax-preferred saving or moving to a consumption tax, these options would raise national saving as much or more, and would be more progressive (Gale, Iwry, and Orszag 2005).

Improve Administration. An intelligent tax reform would equip the Internal Revenue Service with the resources it needs to enforce and administer the system. Many taxpayers simply do not pay taxes they actually owe, while the IRS lacks the resources to enforce payment. Providing the IRS with additional resources generally would boost revenues, provided the money is put to enforcement. At the same time, one can only go so far in this direction, as the additional manpower used reduces net product in the economy as a price for producing a fairer distribution of the tax burden.

Meet Government Spending Needs. Given the spending trends noted above, serious thought needs to be given to the best way to structure taxes designed to raise *additional* revenues. Note that higher revenue needs make it even more important to keep rates as low as possible and the base as broad as possible. I do not think we can extract another 5 to 10 percent of GDP in revenues out of the current individual and corporate income tax system. The needed changes would raise rates too high to be economically sound or politically viable.

One possibility for added revenue, especially if income tax rates are held at 35 percent, would be to apply a Social Security tax at 3 percent on all earnings above the current earnings cap, similar to Medicare's 2.9 percent rate.

Other options involve new taxes. One possibility here—one where there is very strong evidence that it can be administered—is a VAT. A broad-based VAT, one with only a few exclusions, would generate revenue of about 0.6 percent of gross domestic product for each 1 percentage point of tax. It would also increase the cost of government purchases and reduce the income tax base. The net contribution to deficit reduction, therefore, would be about 0.4 percent of GDP for each 1 percentage point of tax. On net a 10 percent VAT, then, could raise an additional 4 to 5 percent of GDP in revenue if the VAT tax base were kept fairly broad. The great advantage of a VAT over a national retail sales tax is that the VAT is a proven collection system in force in more than one hundred countries around the world. Exporters could follow established procedures for getting rebates at the border. Unlike the retail sales tax, the VAT does not have great difficulty in taxing services, as opposed to goods. One form of VAT uses credits that effectively reduce the amount of cheating by requiring users of inputs to make up for missing VAT if their input suppliers have not paid them. Administrative concerns make the NRST a much more iffy proposition, even as a supplement to the existing system.

The VAT could even be earmarked to cover Medicare and Medicaid costs, offering the public a natural way to check its own enthusiasm for ever-higher health-care spending.

Another option would be a tax on, or market in, carbon emissions, which would likely raise significantly less revenue than a VAT. It raises issues in environmental policy that are well beyond the scope of this chapter, but merits serious consideration.

Conclusion

Tax reform is an opportunity to focus on several broader issues that tend to get lost in everyday discussions and politicking. First, the *level* of revenues society is willing to collect should be consistent with the level of government services society would like to provide. Second, the *structure* of revenues should be more consistent in the way it treats assets and debt. Third, a major tax reform is perhaps the only opportunity society will have for a long period of time to make simplification a guiding focus of policy changes and to clean special provisions out of the code. A reform consistent with these three items and not unduly regressive or progressive would not only command substantial political support, but it would also improve the operation of the tax system and the economy.

References

Aaron, Henry J., and William G. Gale. 1996. Introduction. In Henry J. Aaron and William G. Gale, eds. *Economic Effects of Fundamental Tax Reform*, 1–28. Washington, D.C.: Brookings Institution Press.

Aaron, Henry J., William G. Gale, and James Sly. 1999. The Rocky Road to Tax Reform. In Henry J. Aaron and Robert D. Reischauer, eds. *Setting National Priorities: The 2000 Election and Beyond*, 211–66. Washington, D.C.: Brookings Institution Press.

Altig, David, Alan J Auerbach, Laurence J. Kotlikoff, Kent Smetters, and Ian Walliser. 2001. Simulating Fundamental Tax Reform in the United States. *American Economic Review* 91, no. 3:574–95.

Bell, Elizabeth, Adam Carasso, and C. Eugene Steuerle. 2005. Retirement Saving Incentives and Personal Saving. *Tax Notes* 105, no. 13:1689.

Burman, Leonard E., William G. Gale, and Jeffrey Rohaly. 2003. The Expanding Role of the Alternative Minimum Tax. *Journal of Economic Perspectives* 17, no. 2:173–86.

Engen, Eric M., and William G. Gale. 1996. The Effects of Fundamental Tax Reform on Saving. In Aaron and Gale, *Economic Effects of Fundamental Tax Reform*, 83–111.

Gale, William G. 1999. The Required Tax Rate in a National Retail Sales Tax. *National Tax Journal* 52, no. 3:443–57.

Gale, William G., and Janet Holtzblatt. 1997. On the Possibility of a No-Return Tax System. *National Tax Journal* 50, no. 3:475–97.

Gale, William G., J. Mark Iwry, and Peter R. Orszag. 2005. The Automatic 401(k): A Simple Way to Strengthen Retirement Savings. *Tax Notes* 106, no. 10:1207–14.

Gale, William G., and Brennan Kelly. 2004. The No New Taxes Pledge. *Tax Notes* 104, no. 2:197–209.

Gale, William G., and Peter R. Orszag. 2003. The Administration's Proposal to Cut Dividend and Capital Gains Taxes. *Tax Notes* 98, no. 3:415–20.

———. 2004a. Bush Administration Tax Policy: Revenue and Budget Effects. *Tax Notes* (October 4): 105–18.

———. 2004b. Bush Administration Tax Policy: Effects on Long-Term Growth. *Tax Notes* (October 18): 415–23.

Graetz, Michael J. 2004. 100 Million Unnecessary Returns: A Fresh Start for the U.S. Tax System. *Yale Law Journal* 112:263–313.

Hall, Robert E., and Alvin Rabushka. 1995. *The Flat Tax*. Stanford, Calif.: Hoover Institution Press.

McLure, Charles E., Jr., and George R. Zodrow. 1996. A Hybrid Approach to the Direct Taxation of Consumption. In Michael J. Boskin, ed. *Frontiers of Tax Reform*, 70-90. Stanford: Hoover Institution Press.

Rivlin, Alice, and Isabel Sawhill. 2005. *Restoring Fiscal Sanity: Meeting the Long-Run Challenge*. Washington, D.C.: Brookings Institution Press.

Tax Policy Center. 2003. Historical Payroll Tax vs. Income Tax. http://www.taxpolicycenter.org/ TaxFacts/TFDB/TFTemplate.cfm?Docid=230

3

A Fair and Balanced Tax System for the Twenty-first Century

Michael J. Graetz

Who Will Step Up?

President Bush has made clear that he intends to fulfill his campaign promise to "lead a bipartisan effort to reform and simplify the federal tax code," and he has appointed a panel cochaired by former senators John Breaux (D-La.) and Connie Mack (R-Fla.) to suggest options. But many in Washington are betting that major changes won't happen, and tax lobbyists—including some with close connections to the administration and Republicans in Congress—are working to make sure that they don't.

Two decades ago, many similar forces were just as sure that Ronald Reagan's tax reform plan had little chance. President Bush should take a page from Reagan's playbook: He should invest as much of his own time, energy, and political capital in tax reform as he did in securing the tax cuts of his first term. And he must, as Reagan did, try to forge a bipartisan consensus. True bipartisan support is essential to obtain a genuine tax reform that has any hope of lasting.

The smart money is against tax reform, as always. In 1986 the smart money bet against tax reform until the night before the new law was enacted. So the smart money doesn't always win. Beating it, however, demands extraordinary leadership from both the White House and Capitol Hill. In 1986, in addition to President Reagan's personal efforts, crucial leaders emerged in Congress from both sides of the aisle. The legislative proposals of Democrats Bill Bradley and Dick Gephardt and of Republicans Jack Kemp and William Roth, while different, pointed the way to the income-tax reform that actually happened. And Republican Senate Finance Committee chairman Bob Packwood and Democratic Ways and Means Committee chairman Dan Rostenkowski supplied essential leadership in passing the legislation. The key question is whether members of Congress will step up this time.

The tax-policy debate between Democrats and Republicans so far offers reasons for pessimism. Democrats seem to be looking to cut taxes of the poor, to provide tax breaks to the middle class for this or that expenditure, and to raise taxes for high-income people. Many Republicans seem to be looking mostly to provide more tax cuts for savers and investors, who tend to be those with higher incomes. The 1986 tax-reform coalition of supply-side Republicans and tax-reforming Democrats, which produced the revenue-neutral, distributionally neutral, rate-lowering, base-broadening tax-reform legislation signed by Ronald Reagan, has come completely unglued. Tax legislation during the 1990s completed the unraveling of the 1986 Tax Reform Act, which had promised, but failed to deliver, a better and simpler income tax. Republicans seem to favor a narrower tax base with low rates, Democrats a different but also narrower tax base with higher rates. Attempting to overhaul the income tax, as in 1986, does not seem a promising path.

The Income Tax Is Badly Broken

I remember decades ago my father taking over our dining room table, sitting there filling out his tax return off and on from about mid-February until April 15 every year. This infuriated my mother for obvious reasons. My father struggled on, viewing his duty to determine how much tax he owed the way Justice Holmes did: as the price we pay for a civilized society.

What has happened since? Substantively, the income tax is a mess. Taxpayers at every income level confront extraordinary complexity. In 1940, the instructions to the Form 1040 were about four pages long. Today the instruction booklet spans more than a hundred pages, and the form itself has more than ten schedules and twenty worksheets. The Internal Revenue Code contains more than 700 provisions affecting individuals and more than 1,500 provisions affecting businesses—a total of more than 1.4 million words—making the tax law four times larger than *War and Peace* and considerably harder to parse. The regulations contain

FIGURE 1

TAX CODE COMPLEXITY

(approximate words in Internal Revenue Code and regulations)

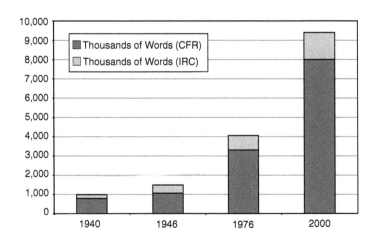

SOURCE: Calculations based on U.S.C. (1940, CCH 1952) and C.F.R. (1940, 1949) and Tax Foundation calculations, based on West's Internal Revenue Code and Federal Tax Regulations (1975), U.S. Congress (2001).

another 8 million words, filling almost 20,000 pages (see figure 1). And both the code and regulations grow fatter every year.

In America today, very few people share my dad's attitude toward taxes. Many feel like "chumps" if they pay the taxes they legally owe. Young people, especially, admit that they feel no compunction about filling out their tax forms dishonestly. And the Internet has facilitated growth of the "tax deniers" movement—people who spread their rejection of the legitimacy of any income-tax requirements, including the requirement for employers to withhold taxes on their employees' wages. When the IRS shuts down one Internet site, more replace it.

We are moving inexorably toward a crisis of compliance with our income tax. Filing a tax return no longer links the American people to their government. Instead, it is just one more commercial operation. H&R Block, Jackson-Hewitt, Turbotax, and a legion of accountants sit between Americans and their government.

Congressional Republicans and Democrats, along with every president, now use income-tax incentives the way my mother employed chicken soup, as a magic elixir for every economic or social ill. If the nation has a problem in access to education, child-care affordability, health-insurance coverage, retirement security, or the financing of long-term care, to name just a few, an income-tax deduction or credit is supposedly the answer.

The competition to give tax breaks for this or that expenditure has badly broken the income tax. It is way too complicated; estimates suggest ordinary citizens and businesses waste about $125 billion every year—thirteen cents for every dollar collected—trying to comply with it, or to avoid it (Slemrod 2005).

At the same time, the Internal Revenue Service is now incapable of administering and enforcing the income-tax law. The fundamental problem is that it is being asked to do too much. Having to administer the earned-income tax credit (EITC)—the nation's wage subsidy for low-income workers—has diverted IRS audit resources away from corporate and high-income individual returns, leading to headlines that the agency is targeting the poor for audits. The IRS routinely processes more than 130 million individual and corporate income tax returns and nearly 1.5 billion information documents each year. It is also supposed to issue regulations promptly implementing frequent and massive legislative changes, to ferret out and deter income-tax protesters and corporate tax shelters, to halt tax evasion, and to bring the underground economy to the surface. The IRS cannot do all of these things well. Many it cannot do at all.

Then there is the train wreck coming down the tracks. The AMT, the alternative minimum tax, if left unchanged, will soon be imposed on more than 30 million Americans. Tens of millions of people will have to struggle to calculate twice—with different rates and different bases—what income tax they owe. The cost of fixing this problem—perhaps $1 trillion over ten years—is why Congress, since 2001, has simply postponed it. The pony in this manure is that the coming AMT disaster offers politicians a terrific opportunity to make some major improvements in our nation's tax system.

It's not surprising that the American people now say the income tax is the worst tax in the U.S. system. For a long time—until 1978—the income tax was regarded by the American people as the nation's best tax (Graetz 1997).

How can anyone remain optimistic about fixing the income tax without radical surgery? Even those who applauded the 1986 act as a wildly successful tax reform must concede now that this legislation was not a stable solution. Over time, its broad base and low rates have been transformed into a narrower base with higher rates. What the nation needs is a new and better tax system, one that is far simpler, fairer, and more conducive to economic growth.

If tax reformers are truly serious about getting the IRS out of the lives of the American people, they must place tax simplification at the top of the agenda. But in Congress, simplification is not a priority. Democrats are primarily concerned with maintaining a progressive tax system, while many Republican tax-cutters want to eliminate all taxes on wealth and capital income—they say to spur economic growth.

President Bush has said that any tax reform must be revenue-neutral, maintain a progressive tax system, and promote economic growth. He has emphasized that "simplification would be the goal" of any changes to the tax code (Bush 2004). But the specifics of his plan are unknown. Will he propose tinkering with the income tax? Or will he go for a flat-rate tax on what people consume or on wages only, exempting all savings or investment income? Or will Bush propose the favorite plan of some congressional Republicans—complete replacement of the income tax with a national sales tax?

Unfortunately, despite their cleverness, the proposals for broad change that have recently been circulating in the Congress—ideas like the "flat" tax and a national sales tax (which its proponents have somehow labeled the "fair tax")—are essentially unrealistic. They supply nice vehicles for railing against the current system, for making political points, but they fail to offer genuine alternatives. This is no time to play Pollyanna.

The "Flat Tax," a National Sales Tax, and a Progressive Consumption Tax Are Not Realistic Alternatives

Flat-tax advocates trumpet their claim that they would shrink the individual tax return to fit on a postcard. But given Congress's propensity for enacting tax breaks to encourage particular expenditures or activities, it is foolish to believe that a flat tax—which would require all wage earners to file tax returns—would stay flat or simple for very long. The political allure of giving Americans tax breaks for specific expenditures or investments is catnip to both Congress and the White House. The Form 1040 itself could once have fit on a postcard.

Nor does the idea of taxing only people's wages seem likely to sit well with the American public over time. The belief that it is unfair to tax only wages and not income from wealth is what led this country to add the Sixteenth Amendment to our Constitution.

Politically, the flat tax's greatest weakness is its treatment of exports and imports—taxing exports, while exempting imports—which makes it anathema to American businesses.[1] Notwithstanding economists' widespread agreement that exchange-rate adjustments will offset this disadvantage, American producers will not stand for a consumption-based tax reform that taxes U.S. production, no matter where the goods are consumed, but fails to tax foreign production of goods consumed in the United States. Its treatment of international commerce—which is required under the General Agreement on Tariffs and Trade (GATT)—is alone enough to doom the flat tax politically.

Proponents of replacing the income tax with a national sales tax have labeled their proposal the "fair tax" and are spending millions of dollars to build grass-roots support. And quite a few congressional Republicans have cosponsored legislation endorsing this idea. But there is no reason to believe that any government can collect a retail sales tax at the high rates necessary to replace the income tax completely. Only six countries have ever adopted retail sales taxes at rates of 10 percent or more; none currently exists (Slemrod 2005). The temptations for retailers to pocket the money are just too great. This is why more than a hundred nations have instead adopted value-added taxes, which are similar to sales taxes economically, but are collected at all stages of production.

Like the flat tax, the national sales tax plan would undermine both private employer-based pensions and health insurance. By eliminating any incentives for either, it would threaten employers' provision of both, which is how most families get their retirement savings (other than Social Security) and their health-insurance coverage. Both of these plans would also eliminate any incentives for charitable contributions or home ownership, contrary to President Bush's insistence that such benefits be retained.

But despite its serious shortcomings, do not underestimate the political forces behind this so-called "fair" tax movement. They resemble the forces that started the effort to repeal the estate tax in the early 1990s. We now know that the failure to take such a political movement seriously can be very costly to its opponents (Graetz and Shapiro 2005).

Since all reporting of sales taxes would be done by retail businesses and no individual returns would be required, a national sales tax would offer genuine simplification for American families. The rub, however, is that complete replacement of the income tax with a national sales tax would provide a large tax reduction for the country's wealthiest people. Like the flat tax, a national sales tax that completely replaces the income tax would unacceptably shift the tax burden away from those with the greatest ability to pay to families with less income. This plan is simply not fair. But there is no "truth-in-labeling" requirement in politics.

Thirty years ago, Dan Throop Smith, a Harvard economist who had served as the Treasury Department's top tax adviser during the Eisenhower administration, accepted the invitation of his daughter, a teacher, to visit her one-room school in Montana. To get a better handle on tax equity, Smith asked three children what would be a fair tax on a family with an income of $5,000, if a family with an income of $2,000 paid a tax of $200.

The first child said, "Five hundred dollars," thereby showing a predisposition for proportional burdens and perhaps a desire to make use of a newly acquired familiarity with percentages. A second child immediately disagreed, adding the comment that the payment should be more than five hundred dollars because "each dollar isn't so important" to the family with the larger income. A third child agreed with the second, but with the reservation that the additional tax over five hundred dollars shouldn't be "too much more or they won't work so hard." Smith subsequently relayed this story in a scholarly article, adding: "Elaborate theoretical structures concerning diminishing utility and incentives and disincentives are all really refinements of the quasi-intuitive opinions of those children and may not lead to any greater certainty" (Smith 1968).

Shortly after the publication of my book, *The Decline (and Fall?) of the Income Tax*, which retells Smith's story, my daughter's fifth-grade teacher asked me to visit her classroom to talk about it. While there, I repeated

Dan Throop Smith's experiment. I asked Smith's question, exactly as he had, and, remarkably, the first three students to speak gave the identical answers in exactly the same order. The intuitions about progressive taxation of children of the late 1990s in a large New Haven, Connecticut, school mirrored precisely those of the Montana children in the 1960s. After I told them that they had given exactly the same answers in exactly the same order as did children more than three decades earlier in a one-room Montana schoolhouse, a number of them wrote to me remarking how "cool," "neat," "amazing," and "weird" that was. One concluded, "I guess that must be fair, if both of the schools got the same answers."

These two experiments should serve as a caution to those who believe that the American public will view as fair replacing a progressive tax on income with a flat-rate tax on consumption. That sentiment will last only until the second child speaks.

The current income tax is a horrible mess. But in the course of radically restructuring our tax system, we should not enact a massive tax reduction for the country's wealthiest people—those who least need such relief—while increasing taxes for those with less income or wealth.

To avoid such a shift in tax burdens, while making the tax system more favorable to savings, Republican senator Pete Domenici and Democratic senator Sam Nunn in the 1990s offered a combination of a value-added tax on businesses and a progressive individual consumption tax as a replacement for the income tax. The Nunn-Domenici plan foundered, however, because of its inability to solve problems of transition from an income tax to the progressive consumption tax and its failure to tax consumption financed with borrowing. In combination, these two problems allowed people with assets or the ability to borrow to avoid the tax (Ginsburg 1995; Warren 1995). The personal tax was essentially a personal tax on wages, but by borrowing for consumption and reinvesting the proceeds of asset sales, people could have sheltered even the wage tax. Senators Nunn and Domenici also concluded that it was necessary to retain a number of existing income-tax preferences, including, for example, the exemption for interest on state and local bonds. This created additional opportunities to consume tax-free. The Nunn-Domenici experiment suggests that enacting a coherent progressive personal tax on consumption is probably not politically viable. This is hardly surprising, since no other nation relies on such a tax.

There are many other tax-restructuring options. The Committee for Strategic Tax Reform, led by Ernie Christian and Gary Robbins, for example, has proposed what it calls five easy pieces: (1) lowering capital-gains rates, (2) eliminating the double tax on corporate earnings, (3) allowing 100 percent of business investment to be expensed, (4) expanding Roth-type IRAs for savings, and (5) moving to a territorial corporate tax that exempts all foreign income.[2] Like the other ideas I have described, this plan would remove tax burdens on wealth or income from wealth and shift burdens to labor income. The reason these particular changes seem easy to their proponents is that they involve only incremental changes in the income tax, and every one of these pieces, except the last, is a major revenue-loser. Like virtually all income-tax proposals, they offer little promise of genuine simplification. They also are targeted to benefit higher-income people and corporations. Their proponents never describe how they plan to pay for these changes—how to offset the revenue losses—because if they did, these "easy pieces" would become a good bit harder to enact.[3] Perhaps we are simply supposed to have faith that increases in economic growth will take care of this new, large revenue hole.

A Fair and Balanced Tax System for the Twenty-first Century

We can achieve low tax rates and a much simpler tax system by replacing most of the income tax with a tax on consumption. In the process, we should return the income tax to its pre–World War II status—a low-rate tax on a relatively thin slice of higher-income Americans. Whittling down the income tax could be financed by enacting a value-added tax (VAT), a consumption tax commonly used throughout the world. A VAT imposed at a 10–14 percent rate could finance an exemption from income tax for families with $100,000 of income or less and would allow a vastly simpler income tax at a 25 percent rate to be applied to incomes over $100,000. In combination, these two taxes would produce revenues roughly equivalent to the current income tax (see table 1).[4] And this proposal, unlike the "flat tax," the "fair tax," and other such proposals, is essentially distributionally neutral. It would not dramatically shift the tax burden away from high-income families to middle- and lower-income families. Also, rather than relying on tax structures like the flat tax and progressive consumption taxes, which were invented in ivory towers and are largely untested in today's economy, this plan combines two of the world's most common tax mechanisms, while exploiting our nation's substantial economic advantages.

Here's the proposal. It contains four pieces, but I don't claim they are easy.

The Individual Income Tax. Increase the AMT exemption for married couples to $100,000 ($50,000 for singles), and index the exemption for inflation so we never find ourselves back in the position we are in today. Lower the AMT rate to 25 percent and repeal the regular income tax. Everybody seems to want to repeal the AMT; let's repeal the regular income tax instead.[5]

This would free about 150 million people from filing income-tax returns. They would have no dealings at all with the IRS. A low flat rate of tax would be imposed on the taxable income of high-income individuals. The income tax that would remain for high-income taxpayers would be shrunken and simplified substantially. The marriage penalties of the existing income tax would be eliminated. Most of the special income-tax credits and allowances that now crowd the tax code and complicate tax forms would be repealed. But the deductions for charitable contributions, home-mortgage interest, and large medical expenses would be retained. In addition, employers would continue to have income-tax incentives to provide their employees with retirement savings plans and health insurance. If Congress desires, a deduction could be allowed for state and local taxes. Congress could tax capital gains at the standard 25 percent rate or maintain a lower rate. Likewise, Congress could retain the special 15 percent rate on dividends or adopt the original 2003 proposal of President Bush, eliminating dividend taxes completely when corporate taxes are paid.

The Corporate Income Tax. Lower the corporate rate to 25 percent, and more closely align book and tax accounting. Only with greater book-tax conformity will we ever really solve the tax-shelter problem that has plagued the corporate income tax for decades.

An identical corporate and top individual rate, along with fewer differences between book and tax measurements of income, would allow major simplification of business taxation. Where Congress wants to

TABLE 1

ILLUSTRATIVE SUMMARY OF REVENUES

Proposal to Revise Individual Income Tax and AMT

Summary of Rates and Balances at 13% VAT (billions of dollars):

	Calendar year			
	2003	2004	2005	2006
1 10% VAT	565	596	628	661
$100,000 individual income tax exemption/AMT base/25% rate[a]	−577	−601	−640	−655
2 2% VAT	113	119	126	132
Replace EITC	−36	−36	−37	−38
Additional funds for tax relief for low- and moderate income families[b]	−77	−83	−89	−94
3 1% VAT	57	60	63	66
Base broadening[c]	58	58	83	81
Corporate rate reduction to 25%	−88	−89	−117	−117
4 13% VAT total rate net	15	24	17	36

SOURCE: Graetz (2002).
NOTE: These estimates were prepared for a seminar delivered to the U.S. Treasury Office of Tax Policy in August 2002. The Treasury's Office of Tax Analysis assisted in the development of these estimates in connection with that seminar. The proposals are assumed to be effective January 1, 2003. The sunset of the 2001 act, scheduled for 2011, is assumed to be repealed. These estimates do not include any potential interactions among proposals. They have not been updated to reflect economic or policy changes since 2002 and are therefore made available here for illustrative purposes only.

maintain book-tax differences, such as for depreciation, research and development expenses, and foreign taxes, these differences would be made explicit. The corporate alternative minimum tax would be repealed. By adopting identical tax rates under the individual and corporate income taxes, the income of small corporations could be taxed on a flow-through basis, thereby eliminating the separate corporate tax for many small businesses and taxing their income directly to their owners. This would allow small-business income to qualify for the $100,000 income-tax exemption, and the taxation of small-businesses could be greatly simplified. The corporate income tax would apply only to large, publicly held companies.

			Calendar year			
2007	2008	2009	2010	2011	2012	2003–2012
696	731	768	807	848	891	7191
−694	−732	−779	−826	−878	−938	−7320
139	146	154	161	170	178	1438
−39	−41	−42	−44	−44	−44	−401
−100	−105	−112	−117	−126	−134	−1037
70	73	77	81	85	89	721
75	79	78	75	74	77	738
−113	−117	−118	−117	−117	−121	−1114
34	34	26	20	12	−2	216

a. The proposal would (1) repeal the regular individual income tax, (2) increase the AMT exemption to $50,000 (singles) and $100,000 (joint returns), (3) index the AMT exemption, (4) lower the AMT rate to a flat 25%, and (5) phase out the AMT exemption at $20 for every $100 in excess of $100,000 (singles) and $200,000 (joint returns). (The current AMT phase-out is $25 for every $100 over $112,000 [singles] and $150,000 [joint returns].) Further broadening the AMT base could reduce the revenue cost of this change.

b. Assumes 2 percentage points of VAT devoted to relief for low- and moderate-income families.

c. A substantial portion of this cost might be funded by broadening the base of the corporate tax.

Enact a Value-Added Tax. To replace the revenues just lost, enact a value-added tax at a 10–14 percent rate. A VAT has effects similar to a sales tax, but a value-added tax is collected at all stages of production, so it is difficult to evade. This is a realistic tax used by more than 120 countries on five continents.

Businesses with gross receipts of less than $100,000 annually (which account for nearly 80 percent of the country's 25 million businesses) should be exempt from collecting VAT or filing returns. Such an exemption would reduce the number of VAT returns to about 5.5 million. An exemption for small businesses would also relieve them from the costs of compliance and the tax collector from chasing after small amounts of tax. European VATs tend to impose compliance costs about one-fourth to one-third as large as our income tax (Slemrod 2005).

In order to keep the tax rate as low as possible, the VAT tax base should be broad, covering nearly all goods and services. A broad VAT tax base with a single tax rate would minimize its economic distortions, and limiting exemptions would simplify compliance and administration.[6] Expenditures on education and religion would be exempt from the consumption tax, as would much expenditure for health care. However, rather than exempting food or clothing, as many foreign VATs and state sales taxes do to reduce the tax burden on necessities, low-income people should be protected from tax increases through an offset of their payroll-tax liabilities.[7]

Many countries that have enacted value-added taxes do not require retailers to state separately the amount of tax imposed on the goods they sell; the tax is buried in the price of products. But this weakness is easily cured by Congress's simply requiring that the total amount of tax be separately stated whenever goods or services are sold.

There are various methods for imposing and collecting such a consumption tax. The best alternative is a so-called credit- or invoice-method VAT of the sort used predominantly throughout the Organisation for Economic Cooperation and Development (OECD) nations.[8] Experience demonstrates that such a tax works well. Sellers of goods and services collect taxes and receive credits for VAT paid on their purchases. This allows tax revenues to be collected regularly throughout the year from companies at all levels of production, rather than just from retailers, thereby easing enforcement (Ebrill et al. 2001, 15, 20). A credit-method VAT also facilitates exemptions for small businesses (and for specified goods or services if such exemptions become politically necessary). The key point is this: The consumption tax should be collected only from businesses, and the tax should be imposed on a broad base at a level sufficient to free the vast majority of Americans both from any income-tax liability and from any requirement to file tax returns.

Provide a Refundable Payroll-Tax Offset. Replace the earned-income tax credit and protect families with low and moderate income from any increased tax burden under this plan through a refundable payroll-tax offset. Providing low- and middle-income workers offsets through the payroll-tax withholding system would allow tax returns to be eliminated for these workers without increasing their taxes, while maintaining the EITC wage subsidy. Moreover, payroll tax offsets would put money in low-income workers' pockets when their paychecks are earned rather than through a lump-sum tax refund after year-end, as the EITC now does.

For several reasons, it is not appropriate that this tax relief correspond precisely to that provided by the current EITC. The EITC now contains serious penalties on marriage, which should not be replicated in any new system, and noncustodial parents are now treated as if they have no financial obligations to their children. Further, for families with children, relief greater than that provided by the EITC will be needed to off-set any new tax burdens created by a consumption tax. This tax relief and wage subsidy for low-income workers would be administered by having employers adjust their employees' paychecks to provide additional take-home pay. The total amount of the adjustment would depend on how many children the worker has. To avoid an abrupt termination of relief with atten-dant high marginal tax rates on wages, families with children might be eli-gible for some tax offset with wages up to about $50,000.

Calculating this offset to payroll-tax withholding would not burden employers; tables would be provided by the IRS showing the amounts of the payroll-tax offsets at different wage levels and family sizes. Employees whose payroll-tax obligations are not sufficient to cover the adjustment would receive a direct increase in their take-home pay.

Although this take-home pay increase for low-income workers takes the form of a reduction of payroll-tax deposits, like the current EITC it would not affect employees' Social Security benefits or the amounts credited to the Social Security Trust Fund. It would be funded from general revenues provided by the VAT. (About 2 percent of a 14 percent VAT would be dedicated to this purpose.) Each employee's wages would be reported to the Social Security Administration in full, thereby providing all necessary information to main-tain the employee's full eligibility for Social Security benefits.

Conclusion

This plan is fair and balanced. It is fiscally sound, designed to maintain current federal government revenues. Unlike proposals to replace the income tax completely with either a "flat tax" or a national sales tax and some other proposals, this plan does not entail a substantial tax cut for high-income individuals, or a tax increase for those below the top tier.

This tax system would make the United States very similar to the average of OECD countries in taxing consumption relative to GDP and in terms of tax rates on consumption (see figures 2 and 3).

Our income tax, however, would be very much smaller—and could be very much simpler—than what people generally face abroad (see figure 4).

This new tax system would have a number of important advantages:

- It would eliminate about 100 million of the 135 million income-tax returns that are now filed (see figure 5). One hundred fifty million people would no longer have to file tax returns. For them, April 15 would just be another day.

- It would be far more favorable for savings and economic growth. Most Americans would owe no tax on savings, and taxes on savings and investment would be lower for everyone. We would also maintain incentives for employers to provide both health-insurance and retirement-savings plans for their employees. The United States would be an extremely attractive place for corporate investments of both U.S. citizens and residents as well as foreigners. This plan should stimulate economic growth and create additional jobs for American workers, producing substantial long-term benefits for the American economy.

- It would eliminate all marriage penalties, something that Congress has so far been unable to do under the current income tax.

- It would not only give the United States a substantial economic leg-up in the world economy, but does so by combining taxes commonly used throughout the world. This system would facilitate international coordination and would fit well within existing international tax and trade agreements.

- It would avoid the difficult issues of transition to an entirely new system that have haunted other proposals to move away from reliance on the income tax.

FIGURE 2

CONSUMPTION TAXES (VAT AND SALES TAX) AS A
PERCENTAGE OF GDP: 2002

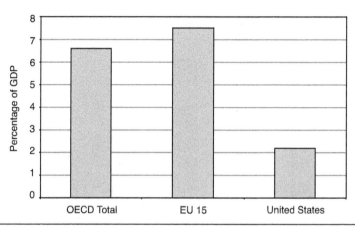

SOURCE: OECD (2004, release 1).

FIGURE 3

CONSUMPTION (VAT) TAX RATES IN THE EU, OECD MEMBERS,
AND THE UNITED STATES: 2000 (unweighted rate average)

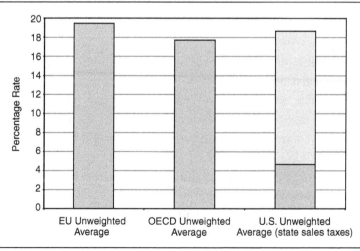

SOURCE: OECD (2001, table 3.5); U.S. computations based on data from http://salestaxinstitute.com
(accessed January 10, 2002).

FIGURE 4

INCOME TAX REVENUE IN THE EU, OECD MEMBERS,
AND THE UNITED STATES AS A PERCENTAGE OF GDP

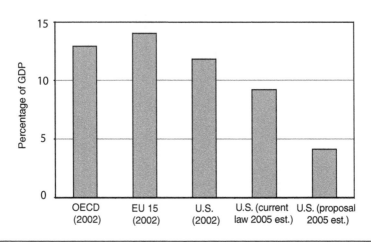

SOURCE: OECD (2004, release 1); U.S. figures for 2005 are author's estimates.
NOTE: OECD reports U.S. revenue for 2003 as 10.9% of GDP.

- It would reduce the IRS workload so that the agency could do its job.

Finally, although Congress will always tinker with the details of taxation, this system promises more stability than the alternatives. I have already said why a pure flat-rate tax on other consumption or income will remain neither flat nor pure for very long. And incremental income-tax changes favorable to savings and investment today will be easy for Congress to reverse tomorrow. Moreover, as long as the vast majority of Americans are required to file tax returns, Congress and future presidents will find irresistible a hodgepodge of tax incentives for this or that expenditure or behavior. This is, after all, how the income tax became the mess it is today. But when the vast majority of families pay their taxes only at the cash register, the political payoff from income-tax incentives will diminish dramatically.

And—short of a major catastrophe—it is hard to imagine any member standing on the floor of Congress urging a reduction in the $100,000

FIGURE 5

TAX RETURNS: CURRENT LAW AND PROPOSAL

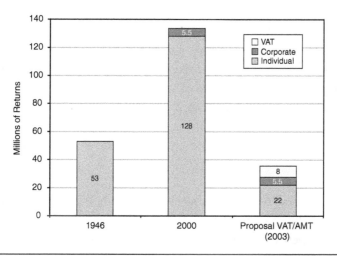

SOURCE: 1946: *Statistical Abstract of the United States* (1956); 2000: Internal Revenue Service Databook (2000); Proposal 2003: Treasury estimates (individual), author estimate (corporate), GAO estimate (VAT). NOTE: GAO has estimated that an exemption for small businesses with gross receipts of $100,000 or less would reduce the required number of VAT returns from 24 million to 5.4 million We assume here that such a small business exemption would be included in a VAT and show 8 million VAT returns filled, since some small businesses will opt into the VAT to obtain refunds and to account for growth since the GAO report was published. *VAT Administrative Costs*, GAO/GGD-93-78 (1993) at 62.

exemption to bring more people into the income tax. Last century, it took World War II for this nation to extend the income tax to the masses. Instead, representatives and senators will be clamoring to get more and more people out from under the income tax.

The greatest threat to the stability of this tax structure is that income or value-added tax rates might rise over time. To protect against the latter, I have urged that we enact a VAT rate high enough (given existing state sales taxes) to leave little room for further increases and use all the money the VAT produces to eliminate income taxation while protecting low- and moderate-income families from a tax increase. For the former, capital mobility in today's global economy offers real protection against individual and corporate income-tax rate increases. The trend around the world is toward lower, not higher, income-tax rates. Some have, nevertheless, expressed concern that with an income tax limited to higher-income tax-payers, the risk of future rate increases grows. But this risk is fully present under the current income tax: Nearly 54 percent of its revenue comes from the top 5 percent of returns with the highest income; nearly two-thirds from the top 10 percent (U.S. Department of the Treasury, Internal Revenue Service 2004). I have also urged enactment of a supermajority voting requirement—60 percent of both the House and Senate—to raise either consumption- or income-tax rates or to lower the income-tax exemption. With this protection, the American people could look forward to a simple, fair, progrowth tax system for the twenty-first century.

Here's what the *Economist* said about this plan in its November 25, 2004, issue:

> Taken together Mr. Graetz's plans imply a wholesale change to America's tax system. That may render them politically unrealistic. Nonetheless, the looming AMT crisis suggests that America has a rare opportunity to clean up its tax code. If he is really serious about reform, Mr. Bush should grasp it.

Notes

1. Most sales or value-added taxes are levied only on consumption that takes place within the country. Exported goods are exempt from the tax. These exemptions are not available under a flat tax, which would tax the entire value of goods manufactured in the United States whether sold here or abroad, but would tax only the U.S. markup of imported goods manufactured abroad. Economists do not regard this as significant because they expect exchange rates to adjust to compensate for this difference. Business owners, on the other hand, perceive a major competitive advantage for imports and will exert their political muscle to oppose such a regime (Graetz 1999).

2. This proposal is detailed in www.nationalreview.com/nrof_comment/conda200409140832.asp.

3. To avoid some of the revenue cost of the "five easy pieces," and perhaps also to prevent the "tax arbitrage" that might otherwise be possible under this plan (Warren and Auerbach 1983), some have suggested combining expensing of business investments with the "comprehensive business income tax" (CBIT) idea for taxing businesses offered by Treasury in 1992 (U.S. Department of the Treasury 1992). With expensing, CBIT may be just another variation of a subtraction-method VAT, along the lines of the flat tax or David Bradford's X Tax (see Bradford's chapter in this volume). Without expensing, CBIT would be a unique form of income tax, taxing interest payments at source rather than residence, unlike any of our tax-treaty partners.

4. For further detail, see Graetz (2002).

5. If the AMT were to serve as the income tax, certain changes would be necessary. For example, expenses of earning income, including employees' business expenses and investment expenses, should be deductible. The $100,000 exemption should make other personal exemptions and credits for children unnecessary. Deductions might or might not be allowed for state and local taxes.

6. A broad, but realistic, consumption-tax base would include approximately half of the nation's gross domestic product, less than the percentage of consumption taxed in some nations, but higher than the OECD average, which is about 40 percent of gross domestic product (Ebrill et al. 2001, 40–42, 43, 46).

7. Alternately, the payroll tax offset might be combined with some VAT exceptions for necessities.

8. A "subtraction-method" VAT, in which value added by each firm is calculated by subtracting allowable purchases from receipts, has often been offered as an alternative. In the United States, this may well be because a subtraction-method VAT looks more like an income tax. Like a credit-method VAT, a subtraction-method VAT must adopt some mechanism to protect low- and moderate-income taxpayers from a tax increase.

References

Bush, George W. 2004. Press Conference Remarks. November 4. www.white house.gov/news/releases/2004/11/20041104-5.html.

Conda, Cesar V. 2004. Five Easy Pieces. *National Review Online*. September 14. www.nationalreview.com/nrof_comment/conda200409140832.asp (accessed April 7, 2005).

Ebrill, Liam P., Michael Keen, Jean-Paul Bodin, and Victoria Summers. 2001. *The Modern VAT*. Washington, D.C.: International Monetary Fund.

Economist. 2004. The Alternative Minimum Tax. November 25.

Ginsburg, Martin D. 1995. Life under a Personal Consumption Tax: Some Thoughts on Working, Saving and Consuming in Nunn-Domenici's Tax World. *National Tax Journal* 48, no. 4 (December): 585–602.

Graetz, Michael J. 1979. Implementing a Progressive Consumption Tax. *Harvard Law Review* 92, no. 8 (June): 1575–1661.

———. 1997. *The Decline (and Fall?) of the Income Tax*. New York: Norton.

———. 1999. *The U.S. Income Tax: What It Is, How It Got That Way, and Where We Go from Here*. New York: Norton.

———. 2002. 100 Million Unnecessary Returns: A Fresh Start for the U.S. Tax System. *Yale Law Journal* 112, no. 2 (November): 261–310.

Graetz, Michael J., and Ian Shapiro. 2005. *Death by a Thousand Cuts: The Fight over Taxing Inherited Wealth*. Princeton: Princeton University Press.

Moody, Scott J. 2000. *The Cost of Complying with the U.S. Federal Income Tax*. Washington D.C.: Tax Foundation.

Organisation for Economic Co-operation and Development. 2001. *Consumption Tax Trends: VAT/GST, Excise and Environmental Taxes*. Paris: Organisation for Economic Co-operation and Development.

———. 2004. *OECD Revenue Statistics*. Paris: Organisation for Economic Co-operation and Development.

Slemrod, Joel. 2005. Testimony before the President's Advisory Panel on Tax Reform, March 3. www.taxreformpanel.gov/meetings/docs/slemrod_03032005.ppt.

Smith, Dan Throop. 1968. High Tax Rate: Inequality or Immorality? *University of Florida Law Review* 20, no. 4 (Spring): 451–63.

U.S. Census Bureau. 1956. *Statistical Abstract of the United States*. Washington, D.C.: U.S. Government Printing Office.

U.S. Congress. Joint Committee on Taxation. 2001. *Study of the Overall State of the Federal Tax System and Recommendation for Simplification*. Washington, D.C.: U.S. Government Printing Office. www.house.gov/jct/s-3-01vol2.pdf.

U.S. Department of the Treasury. 1992. *Integration of the Individual and Corporate Tax Systems: Taxing Business Income Once*. Washington, D.C.: U.S. Government Printing Office. January 6.

U.S. Department of the Treasury. Internal Revenue Service. 2004. *IRS Statistics of Income, September*. Unpublished SOI data available at www.irs.gov/pub/irs-soi/02in01ts.xls.

U.S. General Accounting Office. 1993. *Tax Policy: Value-Added Tax: Administrative Costs Vary with Complexity and Number of Businesses*. Washington, D.C.: U.S. Government Printing Office.

U.S. Internal Revenue Service. 2000. *Internal Revenue Service Databook*. Washington, D.C.: U.S. Government Printing Office.

Warren, Alvin C., Jr. 1995. The Proposal for an Unlimited Savings Allowance. *Tax Notes* 58, no. 9 (August 28): 1103–8.

Warren, Alvin C., Jr., and Alan J. Auerbach. 1983. Comment: Tax Policy and Equipment Leasing after TEFRA. *Harvard Law Review* 96, no. 7 (May): 1579–98.

4

Guidelines for Tax Reform: The Simple, Progressive Value-Added Consumption Tax

Robert E. Hall

This chapter describes how to move down the path toward a simple, progressive consumption tax. It covers improvements that could be made in personal and corporate income taxes, but it does not cover the other major component of the federal revenue system, the payroll tax for Social Security. I have another set of ideas about Social Security, emphasizing its role in financing health care, but that is a topic for another place.

Some of the goals of tax reform command widespread support. The first goal is *simplification*. The personal income tax today is ridiculously complicated. An improved tax would result in a one-page filing for every individual and every business.

The second goal is powerful, uniform *incentives for capital formation*. In today's tax system, entrepreneurial startups are heavily taxed, whereas tax shelters are subsidized. Uniformity of powerful investment incentives is central to a progrowth tax policy.

The third goal is *progressive distribution of the tax burden*. Today's tax system shields the poor from any income tax—a feature that should be retained—but its distribution across middle- and upper-income taxpayers is cruelly uneven. The United States needs an airtight progressive tax.

The fourth goal is *economic efficiency*. Once the other goals are achieved, efficiency calls for moderate top tax rates. Experience worldwide has demonstrated that tax rates above about 30 percent generate inefficiencies that far outweigh the limited revenue that they collect.

Tax specialists have reached a strong consensus that the general answer to the federal government's tax problem is a *consumption tax*. The core of the argument is that an income tax, the only important alternative to a consumption tax, creates a huge inefficiency in the economy. It distorts families' decisions about saving to support future consumption by penalizing future consumption in comparison with current consumption. Yet all taxes cause some kind of distortion. A consumption tax distorts the choice about how much to work in the market, because it taxes the products purchased in the market with the resulting wages, but excuses the time spent at home in enjoyable activities or in nonmarket work. By contrast, the distortion of an income tax is much more serious; it compounds into the future. The income tax is paid year after year on the wealth set aside to finance deferred consumption. The implicit tax rate on consumption twenty to thirty years in the future is almost confiscatory. The harm from an income tax is huge.

In this chapter, I assume that the ultimate goal of tax reform is a national consumption tax, and I suggest how to achieve this goal. Every consumption tax provides the right incentives for capital formation, but consumption taxes differ with respect to the other elements of the specific goals just listed. Not all consumption taxes are simple, not all are progressive, and not all have low, efficient rates.

Comparing National Consumption Taxes

Among consumption taxes, the best choice for the basic structure of the U.S. federal tax system is the *progressive value-added tax* (VAT). The VAT, which is the backbone of the revenue system of every country in Europe, is the essence of simplicity; it provides exactly the right incentive for capital formation, because all investment is deducted from the tax base. The VAT is also efficient, because its rate is in the safe zone below 30 percent. The only defect of the standard European VAT—but a serious one—is its lack of progressivity. European countries complicate their VATs by applying higher rates to luxury goods, but they have not succeeded in achieving a fair distribution of the burden of the VAT. The next section describes how to make a simple VAT progressive without sacrificing any of its desirable features.

Under the European VAT, a business pays a tax on all of its receipts except for export sales. It deducts all of its operating expenses—wages, raw materials, services, and the like. It also deducts its outlays for plant and equipment, research and development, and other forms of capital formation. The only expense not deducted is imported products. The VAT applies to all businesses, not just corporations. The base for the VAT, added over all businesses, is privately generated gross domestic product (GDP) less investment less exports plus imports. Private GDP is consumption plus investment plus exports less imports. Thus the base is just consumption. The VAT is an easy way to place a tax on consumption without measuring each individual's consumption at the personal level.

In the United States, another easy way to tax consumption efficiently without a personal consumption tax return is a *sales tax on consumption goods* sold to U.S. customers. This tax and the VAT treat imports and exports the same way—the tax is not imposed on goods sold to customers outside the United States, but imported consumption goods are taxed, even though they are not U.S.-produced. In principle, the base of the sales tax is identical to the base of the value-added tax. They differ only in that the VAT collects the tax at every stage of production, whereas the sales tax collects only from the business that sells to the final consumer.

Some proponents of tax reform are pushing a federal sales tax. In principle, a sales tax that exempts sales of investment goods has the same benefits as a VAT. But a VAT is much easier to administer than a sales tax. Under a VAT, *every* business pays the tax on all of its sales, whether to other businesses or to final customers. If the customer is a business, the customer deducts the purchase, so there is no double taxation. A seller does not need to keep track of whether its customers are businesses or final customers. Under a sales tax, the seller does need to make that distinction and contend with customers masquerading as reselling businesses when they are actually final customers. Sales taxes are notoriously leaky and cannot sustain tax rates much above 10 percent, so the case against the sales tax is practical. In addition, a sales tax suffers from the same defect as a standard VAT—it is not progressive.

Tax designers have developed a complete, coherent tax system based on personal deductions for saving. Under this *cash-flow consumption tax,* businesses pay no taxes. Households file complex returns that account for all inflows and outflows of cash—the base of the tax is the residual spent on consumption. The cash-flow tax is vastly more complicated and much harder to administer than any form of value-added tax. Because interest in cash-flow consumption taxes has waned, they are not considered further here.

By contrast, a half-century of experience in Europe has proven the feasibility of a VAT. Although there is some variation in rates, tax systems in all of the members of the European Union are quite similar, with most revenue coming from a VAT but with corporate and personal income taxes on top of their VATs. Evasion of the VAT is difficult, because the tax is collected from businesses on their domestic activities. The VAT is an attractive vehicle for fundamental tax reform, but the historical objection to the VAT—and a persuasive one—is that the European VAT is not progressive; it is built into the prices of all the goods bought by low-income families. The European solution to this problem—VAT rates that are lower on necessities than on luxuries—is not adequate. Overall across Europe, the VAT rate is in the 20 percent range, and the tax systems include a progressive personal income tax as well. Some European countries have corporate income taxes at high rates, although the trend is toward reduced corporate rates. Europe sacrifices the efficiency of a pure consumption tax by adding on other features intended to repair the unfairness of a pure VAT.

Canada and some other countries have taken a more satisfactory approach to distributing the burden of their VATs. They pay families a cash rebate of the VAT. The VAT is built into the subsistence level of consumption purchases, but the rebate offsets that part of the VAT and makes it progressive. On net, a family pays no consumption tax at the subsistence level—that is, a family's average tax rate is zero at the subsistence level and rises gradually to the VAT rate as consumption rises. But this approach is limited to the alterations in the distribution of the burden that a single cash rebate can achieve.

In the United States, a cash rebate creates administrative problems, as experience with the earned income tax credit (EITC) has demonstrated. Even for the relatively modest amounts paid to filers under the EITC, fraud has proven rampant. The United States does not maintain a list of citizens who would be eligible for a rebate. Even if there were such a list—and many people oppose such a list on civil liberties grounds—determination of the amount of the rebate would be a nightmare because so many people spend only part of the year in the country. Many recent immigrants move back and forth during the year, and many long-term residents have jobs outside the country.

The Steps to a Progressive VAT

In 1981 Alvin Rabushka and I proposed an improved approach to making the VAT progressive (Hall and Rabushka 1981). This system links the tax rebate to earning wages within the country. It does not require a national register of people eligible for a rebate, and it solves the problem of part-year workers by linking the rebate to actual earnings. Probably most important, it does not pay the rebate in cash—it nets the rebate against part of the VAT. Specialists in tax design have gradually come to recognize what a good idea this is.

Under our approach, the VAT is split into two coordinated taxes. Together, they form a VAT with a generous rebate provision. One part is the tax that falls on all businesses—corporations, partnerships, and single-person proprietorships. It is the same as a European VAT except for two important differences. First, the business tax gives a deduction for compensation (wages, salaries, bonuses, incentive pay, and pensions). Second, a carry-forward is granted at market interest rates for tax losses. The second provision is needed because a rapidly growing business will have a negative tax base as its investment exceeds its cash flow from operations. The VAT does not need a carry-forward, because the lack of a deduction for wages makes a negative base quite rare.

The second part of the progressive VAT design is a personal tax on compensation—it applies to the same compensation items that businesses can deduct. Thus the base for the progressive VAT is the same as that for the standard VAT—all of consumption. The reason for moving the taxation of compensation to the personal level is that the rebate can then be provided as an exemption from the personal compensation tax. Rather than pay taxes and then receive a cash rebate, the taxpayer sees his rebate integrated with the tax.

The Hall-Rabushka administrative setup is part of what is called the flat tax. The name is brilliant marketing, but it fails to convey the central feature of the idea relative to a VAT—the flat tax is progressive because of its rebate feature. The flat tax is flat only on consumption above a designated level, say $40,000 per year for a family of four.

The idea of the flat tax is a single tax rate of 19 percent on all families, above the generous exemption level. But many people now feel—with the dramatic widening of the distribution of consumption over the past three decades among American families—that this single-rate tax schedule does not distribute the tax burden fairly enough. It puts too much of the burden on the middle class and too little on the prosperous. But it would shift the burden in comparison with the current personal tax, which has rates close to 40 percent, starting at upper-middle-class levels.

A tax design to fit the times might have two or even three different tax rates at the personal level. David Bradford advocated this approach to taxation, which he called the X tax (Bradford 2005). The goal of coordination of the two parts of the progressive VAT requires that the business rate and the top marginal rate on compensation be the same. If they are not, high-income taxpayers will craft arrangements that label all of their earnings as business income or compensation, whichever has the lower rate. Those in lower brackets would have the incentive to label income as compensation, which would be explicitly legal and even encouraged.

The following steps would lead to the progressive VAT:

- Eliminate personal taxation of business income: interest, dividends, and capital gains.

- Bring all businesses (partnerships and proprietorships in particular) under the corporate income tax, to be renamed the business tax.

- Remove the deduction for interest in the business tax and remove the personal deduction for mortgage interest.

- Extend depreciation of plant and equipment to first-year write-off.

The result of these reforms would be a progressive VAT, although its administration would differ from that of a standard European VAT. In Europe, the typical family does not have direct contact with the VAT. The tax is embedded in the prices the family pays, but the family does not fill out a personal tax form. The standard VAT cannot therefore be progressive. Under the progressive VAT, families would continue to fill out a personal tax form, but it would be simple enough to fit on a postcard. Only earnings would be reported and taxed. The personal tax would have a generous exemption and could have several rates, say 15 and 25 percent, or 10, 17, and 25 percent.

The progressive VAT would meet all four of the key goals of tax reform. First, it is simple; both the business and personal taxes fit on postcards. Second, it provides exactly the right incentives for capital formation, across the board, through first-year write-off. Third, it is fair because of the exemption and graduated rates in the personal part of the tax. Fourth, it is economically efficient, because its top rate would be no more than 30 percent.

The progressive VAT also would overcome grave inefficiencies in the current income taxes. The central problem is inconsistent incentives for capital formation that result in subsidies for some types of investment and high taxes on others. Incentives to capital formation come in two varieties. The first is depreciation, including first-year write-off. The second is deduction of saving at the personal level. The two have a perverse, inefficient interaction when the business tax permits deduction of interest.

The U.S. Pursuit of Tax Reform

The United States has pursued tax reform along two paths in recent decades. One path is by providing increasingly generous vehicles for tax deferral through designated assets. These vehicles are now available in a large number of forms for retirement and in new forms for college saving and saving for medical emergencies. This reform is thought to overcome the inefficiency of income taxation, which drives a perverse wedge into people's planning for future spending based on current saving. Meanwhile, the nation has pursued tax reform along a second path by lowering the tax rate on the return to capital. Ultimately, the two approaches are redundant. Special tax-deferred vehicles, even if taken to the ultimate form of unlimited tax deferral, would be meaningless in an economy with a true consumption tax, which places no tax on the returns to saving. This point is easy to see in a world in which the only tax is a VAT. Any form of saving has the same benefit as a tax-deferred special account. Fans of true consumption taxation believe that all tax reform efforts should be aimed at moving to a VAT or other consumption tax rather than at proliferating special accounts, though these are a desirable second best if a consumption tax cannot be achieved.

The current tax system is utterly perverse because of the interest deduction at the business level. Huge volumes of funds are deployed every year to exploit the subsidy that occurs when a business borrows and deducts interest but no tax is paid on the interest by the debt holders, which are often pension funds and the holders of individual tax-deferred accounts. When a business finances investment by selling bonds to a pension fund and takes depreciation and the interest deduction on the investment, the investment is inefficiently subsidized. The logic is as follows. One way to achieve an efficient tax system (meaning a true consumption tax) is to let people accumulate wealth in untaxed assets and then apply the tax when the assets are cashed in to finance consumption. The other is to give businesses a write-off for investment. When the tax system grants a write-off—even the partial write-off in current depreciation provisions—and gives deferral, it subsidizes capital formation inefficiently. The interest deduction is central to this inefficiency, because it puts the pension owner in the position of receiving the benefits of the investment without taxation, either at the business level or at the personal level.

One efficient way to run the economy tax-wise is for businesses to operate outside the tax system and for individuals to pay a tax at the time they consume. Another is to give businesses a write-off for investment. The investment financed by debt held by tax-deferred funds gets both. This is the essence of a tax shelter. This problem will become worse if depreciation becomes more generous and the provisions for tax-deferred funds become more generous, as long as business income tax rates remain high and interest is deductible under these taxes. This danger of tax reform is well known to tax specialists, but it has received far too little attention from Congress. By far the best way to eliminate tax shelters is to move to a single, coherent investment incentive.

At the personal level, interest can be deducted against investments financed by borrowing. This deduction would disappear without controversy if the personal taxation of interest and other income from saving were eliminated. Removal of the personal deduction for mortgage interest is also required to achieve a true consumption tax. The political obstacles to that step are formidable.

The central issue in tax reform in the near future will be the choice between evolving toward a VAT or evolving toward a cash-flow tax. Tax reform in recent years has taken steps in both directions, increasing the likelihood of conflicts that create tax shelters that exploit both investment and saving incentives and gain inefficient subsidies. The United States has been adding investment incentives and saving incentives and thus worsening opportunities for tax shelters without coordination.

It is time to move purposely toward the progressive VAT. The reductions in the dividend and capital gains taxes adopted by Congress in 2003 were important steps in that direction. Policymakers made the right choice by reducing the personal rates on these types of income rather than reducing the corporate rates.

The next step should be the elimination of all personal taxation of dividends and business capital gains. The public needs to be educated that these types of income have already been taxed at the business level. Removing personal taxation is not a giveaway to the rich, because the tax on these types of income has already been paid, at the top tax rate, at the business level. The corporate tax is a withholding tax.

Another important step is the rationalization of interest taxation. In some ways, this step is easier, because the removal of interest deductions raises more revenue than is lost from removing taxation of interest at the personal level. The decrease in business interest deductions could be offset by an increase in depreciation, which is discussed shortly. To avoid dislocations, certain transition rules would be needed, but those are not spelled out here.

The big issue in interest taxation and deductions is home mortgage interest. The mortgage deduction is sacrosanct. The deduction could be retained in the progressive VAT setting if there were a special corresponding tax on mortgage interest receipts that recaptured the tax lost from the deduction and maintained the VAT principle overall. Lenders would receive a small incentive to offer alternative mortgages at lower rates that lacked the privilege of interest deduction. The interest on these mortgages would not be taxed when received by the lender. Eventually, Americans would be weaned off deductible-interest mortgages.

The steps taken to move the taxation of all business income to business and to limit personal taxation to earnings should be accompanied by steps to phase in improvements in the depreciation of plant and equipment. After a decade or so, all plant and equipment should be written off for tax purposes in the year of purchase, in accord with the principle of the VAT. During the period of transition, depreciation and write-offs will be higher than normal, because past commitments to depreciation would be honored at the same time that new investment is written off immediately.

At the end of this process will be a progressive VAT. The additional revenue from plugging existing loopholes will permit a top tax rate of about 25 percent for both business and personal taxes. And the tax itself will achieve the four key goals of simplification; uniform, powerful incentives for capital formation; progressive distribution of the tax burden; and economic efficiency.

A perhaps fitting close to this chapter is a list of things the United States should *not* do in pursuing tax reform. It should not consider a national sales tax—it is an administrative nightmare. It should not consider a European VAT—it is not progressive. It should not expand saving incentives at the personal level or make any other changes that anticipate moving to a cash-flow consumption tax—it, too, is an administrative nightmare. The progressive VAT is the desirable goal of tax reform.

References

Bradford, David. 2005. A Tax System for the Twenty-first Century. Chapter 1 in this volume.

Hall, Robert E., and Alvin Rabushka. 1981. A Proposal to Simplify Our Tax System. *Wall Street Journal.* Editorial page. December 10.

5

Would a Consumption Tax Favor the Rich?

R. Glenn Hubbard

Many chapters in this volume discuss the pros and cons of specific options for fundamental tax reform.[1] It is helpful as well to consider the basic sources of efficiency gains from tax reform—income gains of as much as 9 percent (Altig et al. 2001). The bulk of these gains are achieved by reducing the burden of capital income taxation, which arises from the multiple layers of taxation on certain forms of productive business investment. Capital income taxation is also at center stage in the complexity of the present tax system (for example, measurement of capital gains and depreciation and the numbing complexity of tax rules governing multinational companies).

President George W. Bush has pursued an agenda of reducing the efficiency and complexity costs associated with capital income taxation. Yet fundamental tax reform—moving from the current tax system to a broadbased income tax or consumption tax with a simpler structure and lower marginal rates—would be on the watch list for 2005 even without the president's interest. Part of this emphasis reflects the concerns of economists and policy mavens that tax reform could improve the efficiency of the economy and generate extra income for U.S. citizens. But practical factors in the real world of policy debates loom much larger—the perceived declining competitiveness of U.S. firms, the low rates of saving by most Americans, and the growing reach of the alternative minimum tax into millions of middle-income households.

These real-world pressures supported President Bush's tax cuts of 2001, 2002, and 2003. By means of his tax cuts and discussions of tax reform, President Bush has quietly made the case for a simpler tax system that would remove or at least sharply reduce the current-law tax bias against saving and investment. Indeed, the president's framing of the tax reform debate has corralled the real-world pressures for reform into a discussion of a consumption tax as a way of flushing out the familiar "simpler, fairer, fatter" goals of tax reform. And one would hope that this discussion will focus on how to broaden the tax base to make the marginal tax rates on investment (and work and entrepreneurship) as low as possible.

So, if capital income taxation is the "elephant in the room" of tax reform discussions, why is fundamental tax reform so difficult to accomplish? This framing will likely provoke loud outcries that consumption-based tax reform is unfair or, in the language of economists, "regressive." An understanding why these cries are greatly exaggerated reveals not only insight into how tax reform works, but also how it is likely to emerge in the political discussion.

One "fairness" concern about any fundamental tax reform that would broaden the tax base and reduce marginal tax rates is that top rate reductions would benefit only a handful of affluent taxpayers. This "snapshot" distributional analysis calls to mind the imagination of Tevye the Milkman in *Fiddler on the Roof*, who in the song "If I Were a Rich Man" thinks of one staircase for just going up and another for just going down. But in the same way that actual staircases allow for both upward and downward mobility, the tax system sees considerable income and tax rate mobility on the part of households. As a result, the reductions in marginal rates made possible by tax reform would affect many more individuals than a snapshot suggests.

In 2003, the White House Council of Economic Advisers used Treasury Department data on households for the years 1987–96 to study how households change income tax brackets over time (see Council of Economic Advisers 2003, exhibit 5.4). More specifically, the economists used the data to ask what tax rates households would have faced had President Bush's signature Economic Growth and Tax Relief Reconciliation Act of 2001 been in place over this period. The tabulations revealed that more than half of taxpayers were in a different tax rate bracket at the end of the period and that the upward and downward mobility was significant: Two-thirds of taxpayers in the lowest bracket had moved to a higher bracket after ten years, and four times more taxpayers were subject to one of the top two tax rates in at least one of the ten years than was indicated by the initial snapshot.

But the much more significant "fairness" concern about tax reform in the form of a consumption tax is the claim that such a tax would exempt income from saving from tax. To the extent that higher-income and wealthier households save more (both absolutely and relative to their income),[2] a shift to a consumption tax would confer much larger gains to the higher-income and wealthier taxpayers. Such an argument is intuitive— but wrong. A broad-based consumption tax need not be more regressive than a broad-based income tax. The real challenge for tax reform is to accomplish either one.

The "Fairness" of Consumption Taxation

Critics often claim that, as a tax base, consumption is less fair than income, because the benefits of not taxing capital income accrue to high-income households. As is often noted, this claim depends critically on the time frame for analyzing fairness; consumption taxes may be less regressive from a lifetime perspective than from an annual perspective.[3]

The truth is that, despite the common perception that consumption taxation eliminates all taxes on capital income, consumption and income taxes actually treat similarly much of what is commonly called capital income. Not all capital income escapes the consumption tax. In principle, capital income can be decomposed into four components: (1) the risk-free interest rate (the return to waiting); (2) the expected risk premium for investing (the return to risk taking); (3) returns to market power, entrepreneurial skill or ideas (what economists call economic profit); and (4) a remainder that reflects good or bad luck. For most investments, the income tax base—but not the consumption tax base—includes the first component of capital income; both tax bases treat the last three components of capital income similarly. Relative to an income tax, a consumption tax exempts only the tax on the opportunity cost of capital.

I focus here on a set of plausible and widely discussed prototypes of tax reform. Moving from the current U.S. tax base to a broad-based consumption tax base encompasses two reforms: (1) a move from the current income tax to a broad-based income tax with uniform capital taxation (as under the Treasury Department's 1992 proposal of a comprehensive business income tax), and (2) a switch from this pure income tax base to a consumption tax base (as under the flat tax of Hall and Rabushka).[4] The short-run and long-run distributional consequences of moving from the current tax system to a consumption tax may differ in significant ways. In the short run, eliminating differential capital taxation would affect asset prices, favoring assets that are currently heavily taxed, such as corporate capital, over assets that are lightly taxed, such as housing. The short-run effects of switching from an income base to a consumption base may depend heavily on transition rules. And the short-run distributional consequences of changes in asset prices depend critically on the current pattern of assets holding in the economy and the horizon over which different people plan to hold their assets.

A central question for distributional analysis is which savers earn higher returns. For example, for a given level of wealth, investors whose returns mainly consist of risk-free returns on savings would benefit more than investors whose returns include returns to risk taking or rents from entrepreneurial activities. But how many very wealthy taxpayers earned their fortunes by saving up risk-free returns?

Comparison of Income and Consumption Taxes

It is useful to begin by comparing two benchmark taxes: a pure uniform-rate income tax and a subtraction-method value-added tax (or combination of a wage tax and a business cash-flow tax at the same rate). A pure uniform-rate income tax has a base that includes all forms of labor and capital income and a flat rate. This system would tax corporate and noncorporate capital at the same total tax rate. One way to implement such an income tax would be to combine a business-level tax (for both corporate and noncorporate firms) on receipts, less wages, materials costs, and capital depreciation, with a household-level tax on wages. For simplicity, suppose that the business and household taxes are imposed at a flat rate; that the two tax rates are the same; that no tax-favored ways of holding wealth are available; and that the economy is closed to capital flows. Abstracting from risk considerations, the revised income tax system, then, has three components: (1) a wage tax, (2) a tax on returns from break-even investment projects, and (3) a cash-flow tax on returns from existing capital and highly profitable investment projects. Within the context of broad-based income tax reform, Treasury's comprehensive business income tax (CBIT) proposal generally followed this model (U.S. Department of the Treasury 1992).

In a subtraction-method value-added tax (VAT), each business has a tax base equal to the difference between receipts from sales of goods and services and purchases of goods and services from other businesses. This measure of value added is then taxed at a fixed tax rate. Transactions among businesses generate offsetting increases in the tax base of sellers and decreases in the tax base of buyers, so that no net revenue accrues to the government. Net revenue arises when goods are sold by a business to a nonbusiness entity, generally households. Because the aggregate business tax base equals the aggregate sales by businesses to nonbusinesses, the tax base is equivalent to aggregate consumption. As long as tax rates are uniform, this subtraction-method value-added tax is equivalent to the familiar European-style credit-invoice value-added tax.

A uniform tax could be achieved by equivalently allowing a deduction for wages at the business level with wage taxation at the same rate for individuals (as in the Hall-Rabushka flat tax). Thus the VAT can be envisaged as a combination of a wage tax and a tax on business cash flow. With this alternative means of administration, the consumption tax strikingly resembles the benchmark income tax. The difference between the two taxes, if one abstracts from the treatment of losses, is that the income tax base depreciates capital expenditures and the consumption tax base deducts capital outlays.

Riskless Returns to Capital: What Is Taxed? Traditional descriptions of the taxation of capital income under a cash-flow tax or consumption tax assume that all income from capital is exempt.[5] For example, assume that investment projects offer a single riskless rate of return. Then decompose the base of the flat tax into two parts: The first is a business cash-flow tax whose base is $R - I$, where R is receipts from sales of goods and services less purchases for labor, raw materials, and services, and I is expenditure on capital goods.[6] The second is a wage tax, whose base is wages, W. (The subtraction-method VAT combines the two pieces, with a base equal to

$R + W - I$.) The wage tax burden is borne by labor, but who bears the burden of the cash-flow tax?

Under the cash-flow tax scheme, taxes would no longer affect business investment decisions. The present value of one dollar's worth of depreciation deduction would be one dollar, whereas under the income tax the present value is less than one dollar. The present value of depreciation allowances depends on the depreciation schedule prescribed by the tax code for the firm's assets and the discount rate that the firm uses to discount the future tax savings from the depreciation allowances. Hypothetically, depreciation schedules reflect the useful life of different assets. In a riskless investment project, the tax savings from depreciation allowances represent riskless cash flows that the firm would discount at the risk-free rate of interest.

For a break-even investment—one in which the expected rate of return just equals the interest rate—the upfront subsidy to investment provided by expensing just equals the expected future tax payments. *It is only in this sense that the return to capital is not taxed under the cash-flow tax (or, equivalently, under the consumption tax).*

Entrepreneurial Returns: What Is Taxed? The example assumed a single riskless return on investment projects. Now suppose that, in addition to having access to riskless investments, certain entrepreneurs have access to very profitable investments in which profits are associated with ideas, managerial skill, or market power.

Extending the example, what is taxed are rates of cash flow in excess of the riskless rate of return. Cash flows representing entrepreneurial rents are taxed equivalently under the broad-based income tax and the cash-flow tax (or consumption tax). As long as the scale of entrepreneurial projects with rents is limited, the tax savings from expensing should be invested in another riskless asset. For entrepreneurial projects, then, only the component of the return representing the riskless rate is untaxed under the cash-flow tax (or consumption tax).

Risky Investment: What Is Taxed? Introducing risk adds two complications. First, risky investments have a higher required rate of return than riskless investments, reflecting a risk premium to compensate savers for bearing risk. Second, risky investments generate—after the fact—high or low returns to investing. In the actual distribution of capital income across households, some variation reflects this good or bad fortune. The component of capital income that represents luck after a risky investment decision has been made can be treated like the rents in the benchmark income tax and cash-flow tax. Actual realized returns in excess of the expected return are taxed under both the income tax and the cash-flow tax. Assuming similar loss offset provisions, low realized returns also generate the same tax consequences under the two systems.

Whether either tax system levies a tax on the risk premium depends on how one defines a tax. If a tax is defined as an increase in expected government revenues—the definition economists generally prefer—then *both* the income tax and the cash-flow tax include the risk premium. If, by contrast, a tax is an increase in the discounted present value of government revenues, then neither tax system includes the risk premium. This distinction is most easily seen for a cash-flow tax with full loss offsets. By levying such a tax, the government shares equally in the costs and revenues of investment projects. This feature of the tax system prompts the analogy of the government as a "silent partner" in the investment. Suppose that the government taxes two projects with the same costs but with different expected returns (because one project is riskier than the other). Like private investors, the government would expect a higher return on its investment (cost sharing) in the riskier project. However, assuming that the expected returns compensate for the risk, the "market value" of this extra expected revenue would be zero, because it compensates the government for the added riskiness of the revenue stream. There is no free lunch—the government does not increase the discounted present value of its revenue by taxing pure risk.

In contrast to the cash-flow tax, an income tax provides depreciation allowances rather than expensing for capital purchases. This difference does not affect the treatment of the uncertainty about costs and revenues, as long as the two tax systems have similar loss-offset provisions. By providing depreciation allowances rather than expensing, the government pays a smaller share of the cost of investment projects, because the investor recoups the government's "share" of the cost in the future rather than at the time of the outlay. The present value of the loss to the investor (and, conversely, the gain to the government) depends on how the tax savings from depreciation allowances should be discounted. As long as tax rates do not change, the government's promise of depreciation allowances gives the investor a safe, predictable cash flow, which warrants discounting at the default risk-free rate of return. Thus the benchmark income and consumption taxes treat the return to risk taking similarly.

Putting these arguments together, what is often called the return to capital can be thought of as the sum of the riskless return (return to waiting), entrepreneurial returns (economic profits), and a risk premium on risky investments (payment for bearing risk) and realizations on risky investments (luck). Unlike the consumption tax base, the income tax base includes the opportunity cost of capital, which equals the rate of return on a marginal riskless project. Assuming the consumption tax does not change the rate of return on investment, for investments with the same opportunity cost the owner of the investment with a high rate of return will pay more in taxes than the owner of the investment with a lower rate of return. Because households that save benefit from eliminating the tax on the opportunity cost of capital, they benefit from this tax reform. However, because entrepreneurial returns are still taxed, the distributional effects also depend on separating "opportunity cost" returns to saving from entrepreneurial returns and returns to risk taking.

Shifting the Tax Base from Income to Consumption

A major focus of the political discussion of the incidence of a consumption tax is the transitional redistribution accompanying a switch from an income tax to a consumption tax. Within the familiar life-cycle framework, part of the gain in economic well-being accompanying the tax reform is attributed to a transition tax, borne disproportionately by the elderly in the conventional life-cycle setting. The elderly accumulate assets to finance retirement consumption under the income tax regime, but now they must pay tax again on those funds as they are used to purchase goods and services. The extent to which the elderly bear this burden depends on the change in the after-tax price of consumption from switching tax bases. In part, the after-tax price of consumption depends on the general price level effects of tax reform, which, in turn, may depend on the administration of tax reform. If the transition tax stems only from disallowing depreciation allowances and not from a one-time increase in the price level, then the elderly bear the tax only to the extent that they own a disproportionately large share of assets that lose their depreciation allowances. There is another significant consideration, however: Consumption taxes offer higher expected future (after-tax) returns to saving. Thus to the extent that the transition tax is borne by individuals with relatively long future consumption horizons, the consumption tax may make even households bearing the transition tax better off. Yet decomposing capital income into its components suggests that the higher expected future (after-tax) returns to saving applies only to a small component of observed returns.[7]

Eliminating the Differential Taxation of Capital Income

The broad-based income tax assumed by the benchmark described earlier bears only a faint resemblance to the current U.S. tax system. An important difference between the two is the current system's differential taxation of capital income. Most prominent is the double taxation of equity-financed corporate investment created by the existence of a separate corporate income tax (although this bias was reduced by the 2003 tax legislation). Moreover, variation in the generosity of depreciation allowances across assets generates differences in the effective tax rates across investments. In addition to the corporate tax, many provisions of the individual tax code also produce differential taxation, such as differential tax rates on capital gains and dividends, the nontaxation of the implicit returns from consumer durables, the exemption from tax of interest on state and local government bonds, and various provisions to encourage retirement saving.

Again, a consumption tax is only one method of uniform capital income taxation. Such taxation can also be achieved (albeit at a somewhat higher rate) by reforming the income tax system—for example, the Treasury Department's comprehensive business income tax proposal eliminated most of the main forms of differential capital taxation. Thus the distributional issues associated with eliminating differential taxation are not unique to a consumption tax but can apply to income tax reform.

Distributional Consequences of a Consumption Tax

After studying U.S. household-level data, Gentry and Hubbard (1998) concluded that the switch from a pure income tax to a consumption tax is likely to be less regressive than commonly assumed. Despite the claim that consumption taxes do not tax capital income, replacing depreciation allowances with expensing only eliminated the taxation of the opportunity cost of capital and not capital income attributable to rents and luck (either good or bad). Because wealthier households receive a larger portion of what is often called their capital income in the forms treated similarly by income and consumption taxes (realized returns to risk taking and entrepreneurial returns), a consumption tax is less regressive than would be suggested by assuming that a consumption tax exempts all parts of capital income. The distributional analysis by Gentry and Hubbard suggests that more than one-third of the reduction in the share of taxes paid by very high-income households in switching from an income tax to a consumption tax is offset by this effect.

That analysis illustrates the benefits of separating the parts of tax reform inherent to taxing consumption from those associated with a broad-based income tax. For the debate over fundamental tax reform, the advantages and disadvantages of eliminating differential capital income taxation can be separated from the choice between income and consumption as the tax base. Moreover, in some cases the elimination of differential capital taxation may be the more important of the two issues.

Getting There from Here

Large efficiency gains are possible from fundamental tax reforms.[8] Efficiency and simplicity gains for individuals and businesses will be greatest under a consumption tax. The counterclaim that consumption tax reform is a sop to the rich is almost certainly unfair, especially if a progressive consumption tax like that proposed by Bradford in this volume were under consideration.[9] But even abstracting from such considerations, the sense in which the distributional burdens of "textbook" income and consumption taxes are closer than conventionally imagined offers three lessons for the process of tax reform. First, many of the economic gains from fundamental reform can be obtained from reform of the income tax (though additional pro–business investment and prosimplification gains can be achieved by the further shift to a consumption tax). Second, following this observation, as the reform debate unfolds, "fairness" assaults on tax reform will likely take aim at progrowth changes in the income tax—reduced double taxation of savings, in particular. But such tax changes are popular. Finally, should tax reform enter the legislative process, compromises include graduated wage tax rates or a hybrid tax in which capital income is still taxed at the individual level, but at a lower rate than wage income (as is true under the 2003 tax legislation championed by President Bush). The debate on these compromises will, however, return to the question of what types of base broadening will pay for tax reform's lower rates. That seems to be fair.

Notes

1. This chapter was prepared for the American Enterprise Institute Conference on Fundamental Tax Reform, held in Washington, D.C., February 11, 2005. The author is grateful to Alan Auerbach, Kevin Hassett, and conference participants for helpful comments and suggestions.

2. And the empirical evidence suggests that they do—see, for example, Dynan, Skinner, and Zeldes (2004) and Gentry and Hubbard (2004).

3. See, for example, Davies, St. Hilaire, and Whalley (1984); Poterba (1989); and Fullerton and Rogers (1993).

4. See Hall and Rabushka (1983, 1995). Other flat-tax proposals generally modeled on Hall and Rabushka include those by Treasury Secretary Nicholas F. Brady in 1992 and by Rep. Richard K. Armey (Texas) in 1998. The "X tax" proposal of David Bradford (2004) adopts a structure similar to that of the flat tax but allows for multiple tax brackets.

5. This argument is an old one, tracing its roots to John Stuart Mill's evaluation of capital income taxation as inherently representing double taxation. A similar argument appears in Musgrave (1959).

6. The business cash-flow tax has a long pedigree among economists seeking to apply consumption tax principles to business taxation. An early exposition appears in Brown (1948); implementation issues are discussed in King (1975), Institute for Fiscal Studies (1978), and Hubbard (1989).

7. Much of the conventional analysis of the distributional consequences of a shift to consumption taxation emphasizes the "tax on old capital" associated with a "cold turkey" switch from an income tax to a consumption tax. As Gentry and Hubbard (1997, 1998) observe, this effect for equities is overstated. Equity prices should decline by a lesser amount and may even rise modestly in response to a consumption tax reform. This result is particularly likely in cases in which firms require a significant period of time to make new capital investments. In this instance, existing investments earn higher after-tax returns in response to the lower marginal tax rates following tax reform.

Another commonly cited transition cost relates to owner-occupied housing. As Gentry and Hubbard (1997, 1998) note, a switch from the current tax will likely depress house prices in the short run, but only modestly. The largest such declines should be concentrated in regions in which there are many homeowning households with high marginal tax rates, as in California or New York.

8. See Auerbach and Kotlikoff (1987) for an early discussion of these gains, and the introduction to this volume for a description of this literature.

9. Indeed, Altig et al. (2001) find that even the lowest income groups benefit from a switch to an X tax.

References

Altig, David, Alan J. Auerbach, Laurence J. Kotlikoff, Kent A. Smetters, and Jan Walliser. 2001. Simulating Fundamental Tax Reform in the United States. *American Economic Review* 91 (June): 574–95.

Auerbach, Alan J., and Laurence J. Kotlikoff. 1987. *Dynamic Fiscal Policy.* Cambridge: Cambridge University Press.

Bradford, David F. 2004. *The X Tax in the World Economy: Going Global with a Simple, Progressive Tax.* Washington, D.C.: AEI Press.

Brady, Nicholas F. 1992. Remarks Presented at the Graduate School of Business, Columbia University. New York, December 10.

Brown, Edgar Cary. 1948. Business-Income Taxation and Investment Incentives. In *Income, Employment and Public Policy: Essays in Honor of Alvin H. Hansen.* New York: Norton.

Council of Economic Advisers. 2003. *Economic Report of the President.* Washington, D.C.: U.S. Government Printing Office.

Davies, James, France St. Hilaire, and John Whalley. 1984. Some Calculations of Lifetime Tax Incidence. *American Economic Review* 74 (September).

Dynan, Karen, Jonathan Skinner, and Stephen P. Zeldes. 2004. Do the Rich Save More? *Journal of Political Economy* 112 (April): 397–444.

Fullerton, Don, and Diane Lim Rogers. 1993. *Who Bears the Lifetime Tax Burden?* Washington, D.C.: Brookings Institution Press.

Gentry, William M., and R. Glenn Hubbard. 1997. Distributional Implications of Introducing a Broad-Based Consumption Tax. In James M. Poterba, ed. *Tax Policy and the Economy*, vol. 11. Cambridge, Mass.: MIT Press.

———. 1998. Fundamental Tax Reform and Corporate Financial Policy. In James M. Poterba, ed. *Tax Policy and the Economy*, vol. 12. Cambridge, Mass.: MIT Press.

———. 2004. Entrepreneurship and Household Saving. In *Advances in Economic Analysis and Policy* 4 (1).

Hall, Robert E., and Alvin Rabushka. 1983. *Low Tax, Simple Tax, Flat Tax.* New York: McGraw-Hill.

———. 1995. *The Flat Tax.* 2nd ed. Stanford, Calif.: Hoover Institution Press.

Hubbard, R. Glenn. 1989. Tax Corporate Cash Flow, Not Income. *Wall Street Journal.* February 16.

Institute for Fiscal Studies. 1978. *The Structure and Reform of Direct Taxation.* London: Allen and Unwin.

King, Mervyn A. 1975. Current Policy Problems in Business Taxation. In *Bedrifts Beskatring.* Bergen: Norwegian School of Economics.

Musgrave, Richard A. 1959. *The Theory of Public Finance.* New York: McGraw-Hill.

Poterba, James M. 1989. Lifetime Incidence and the Distributional Burden of Excise Taxes. *American Economic Review* 79 (May): 325–30.

U.S. Department of the Treasury. 1992. *Integration of the Individual and Corporate Tax Systems: Taxing Business Income Once*. Washington, D.C.: U.S. Government Printing Office.

6

Political and Economic Perspectives on Taxes' Excess Burdens

Casey B. Mulligan

A better tax system may lead to more wasteful spending.
—Stanley Fischer and Lawrence H. Summers (1989)

The general lesson for those who like large government is that the way to pay for most of it is through a roughly uniform tax on the broad middle class.
—Robert J. Barro (1993)

$E = mc^2$ is a formula resulting from both hard work and genius. It was developed by a pacifist, but used to create the most destructive weapons known to man. Economics has it own ironic story, which is still in progress. Both hard work and genius have helped produce recommendations for new and more efficient tax systems. Many of the producers generally favor small government, but efficient tax systems may have been used to create the largest governments in the world.

Taxes affect behavior. Most reduce efficiency. Although there is disagreement about the details, these basic results have been long and widely recognized among economists and have received serious attention in policy circles, under both Democratic and Republican administrations, that have included but not been limited to the White House, the Treasury, and the Congressional Budget Office. For example, in the absence of taxation, a well-functioning capital market tends to create capital up to the point where the value of owning it (in terms of increasing the owner's standard of living over time) equals the value of using it. The capital market generates this result because users of capital pay the owners, and only the owners, for its use. If there were a tax on capital income, the users of capital would, in effect, pay two parties for its use, namely the owners and the Treasury. Hence, the value of using capital would exceed the value of owning it. Unless the owners of capital cared as much about making money for the Treasury as they did about making money for themselves, they would supply capital up to the point where its cost equaled the value of owning it, which, as we said, is short of the value of using it. This is an example of taxes affecting behavior and reducing efficiency: The capital income tax reduces capital accumulation and prevents capital's being supplied up to the point where the value of owning it equals the value of using it.

Recent work has shown that taxation of capital income significantly reduces growth in consumption and is the primary reason why, in the postwar U.S. economy, the value of using capital exceeded the value of owning it. Figure 1 displays some of the results. The dashed line is the percentage difference between the values of using and owning capital, with the former measured as the pretax rate of profit from the business and housing sectors, and the latter measured according to the rate of increase of real private consumption expenditure.[1] The difference is positive, which represents the idea that capital is worth more to businesses and home dwellers than it costs savers to supply. The difference fell during the late 1960s and the 1970s, and then rose again since the mid-1980s, mainly because business profit rates were falling and then rising again. The solid line shows how rates of capital income taxation tend to coincide with the dashed line.[2]

Correlation does not prove causation, but the economics of taxes suggests that capital income taxes create inefficiency in the capital market by driving a wedge between the value of capital to its users and the costs of supplying it, and figure 1 supports this. Between 1968 and 1983, the corporate income tax rate was cut, investment tax credits were introduced, and depreciation schedules were accelerated, each of which eased the tax burden on capital. The dashed line suggests that the changes in the law increased efficiency in the capital market by bringing the costs of supplying capital closer to the value of using capital.[3] Since 1986, the removal of

FIGURE 1

CAPITAL INCOME TAXATION AND CAPITAL MARKET INEFFICIENCY

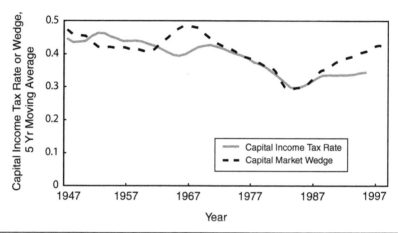

SOURCE: Mulligan (2004).

investment tax credits and accelerated depreciation seem to have more than offset the statutory reductions in tax rates, and thereby increased the rate of capital income taxation. The dashed line shows a corresponding increase in the value of using capital relative to the cost of supplying it.

All taxes, not just those on capital income, create inefficiencies of this general character. A labor income tax causes the value of supplying labor to fall short of the value of using it. A tax on telephone services causes the value of supplying telephone services to fall short of the value of using them, and so forth. The results also imply that a dollar in the Treasury costs the private sector more than a dollar. The private sector, of course, had to sacrifice the dollar, but it also changed its behavior (for example, by working less, or working with an eye toward tax savings rather than economic efficiency) in order to avoid paying yet further taxes. In economics jargon, this is the "excess burden" of taxes. Most economists agree that the marginal excess burden is too large to be neglected, although estimates of it for the personal income tax range from 40 to 200 percent of the incremental revenue (Slemrod 1998). In other words, collecting an additional $1.00 of personal income tax would cost the private sector at least $1.40, and maybe as much as $3.00. Furthermore, tax reformers emphasize how the excess burden depends on the mix of tax instruments used, and how it might be significantly reduced by a shift to a payroll tax, a flat income tax, and/or a VAT tax (Hall and Rabushka 1995).

Democratic and Republican economists agree that the excess burden of taxes is socially wasteful. This is not to say that taxes, or tax increases, are necessarily bad. The excess burden is an additional cost to be considered, and may well be outweighed by the benefits government spending may bring in terms of favorable redistribution, providing public goods, and so on. Of course, people have a variety of opinions as to which kinds of government spending have the greatest benefits. Is education spending one kind? Defense spending? Elderly assistance? Public housing? The space program? Grants for economics professors? Regardless of how you would like the Treasury to spend its money, the existence of the excess burden raises the question of how to minimize it.

Economists have carefully addressed this question for almost a century now, concluding, among other things, that tax loopholes should be minimized, that taxes should be broad-based, that activities that are hard to adjust should be taxed more heavily, and that a good tax system leaves taxpayers some incentives to contribute to the tax base (for example, by leaving marginal income-tax rates below 100 percent). These recommendations, and others, are examples of the calculus of raising the Treasury's revenue in a way that has the least excess burden per dollar collected. They get close attention in policy circles, and were taken quite literally during the tax reforms of the 1980s in the United States and the 1990s in Sweden, and many other tax reforms around the world.

Although it is widely recognized that taxpayers change their personal and business behavior in order to reduce or limit their tax liability, and that their changes are related to the excess burden, not as well recognized is that taxpayers change their political behavior in order to reduce or limit their tax liability. Their political behavior is related to the same excess burden created by their private behavior. It is the political influence of taxpayers that limits the amount of revenue collected by the Treasury, not the technology of tax collection.

For example, table 1 shows how payroll tax rates are double or triple the U.S. level in some European countries. As a result, payroll tax revenues as a fraction of labor income are at least double in France, Germany, and

TABLE 1

AMERICAN GOVERNMENT HAS ROOM TO GROW

Country	Payroll tax rate (%)	VAT rate (%)	Public spending (% of GDP)
France	53.5	19.6	53.5
Germany	48.5	16.0	48.5
Netherlands	47.5	19.0	47.5
United Kingdom	40.7	17.5	40.7
United States	35.7	0	35.7

SOURCE: Tax rate data for 2004 are from the Social Security Administration (2004) and the European Commission (2004). Public spending data are from the OECD (2004), for all levels of government, and are for 2002.
NOTE: The payroll tax rate is calculated as the sum of employer and employee rates, divided by (100 + employer rate).

the Netherlands, and presumably could be doubled in the United States if we adopted their rates of payroll taxation. Table 1 also shows how a national sales tax (or VAT) is important in European countries but so far is an untapped revenue source for the United States. And there certainly are political groups—especially those who would benefit from larger spending programs—who would like to see these revenue increases. Somebody or something in the political sector is stopping them. At least part of the resistance comes from those would who pay new or higher taxes, such as the retail businesses that would pay a sales tax, or employers who would pay higher payroll taxes.

What determines the amount of taxpayer resistance? This is the $2 trillion question, but an answer comes directly out of the aforementioned calculus of excess burdens. Presumably, a taxpayer's resistance to tax hikes rises with the amount the new taxes would cost him, which includes not only the revenues delivered to the Treasury, but also the behavioral changes made by the taxpayer to limit his tax liability. In other words, the growth of government is resisted most when taxes have a heavy excess burden.[4]

Consider a little model of voting on the government budget. The model economy has three types of voter-taxpayers, in equal numbers: those who have potential incomes of, respectively, $10,000, $50,000, and $120,000. A political candidate proposes a public school program that provides $6,000 worth of benefits to each person, which would be financed with a 10 percent income tax. If the tax had no substitution effect on behavior, and thereby no excess burden, two out of three people would vote in favor of it because it costs them only $1,000 or $5,000, depending on their income. Those earning $120,000 would vote against it. If, on the other hand, the income tax had to be levied at a 20 percent rate because taxpayers cut their income-earning effort in half, then the people with $50,000 potential would pay $5,000 in taxes plus something between $0 and $5,000 in excess burden, and therefore might be harmed by the policy proposal.[5] They and those with $120,000 potential would defeat the policy proposal in an election. This is just an example, but it illustrates a general principle that the excess burden of taxes reduces the size of the voting coalition that can benefit from redistribution (Mulligan 2001).

Figure 2 shows the postwar history of federal revenues from the Social Security and individual income taxes, as a ratio to total adjusted gross income (hereafter, AGI). The individual income tax has almost as many cuts as increases, with the most notable cuts resulting (at least in part) from tax-law changes under George W. Bush, Ronald Reagan (twice), Richard Nixon, and John Kennedy, and two tax cuts following the conclusions of World War II and the Korean War. The statutory payroll tax rate has been increased more than twenty times, but it has *never* been cut in its sixty-eight-year history. The tax is capped, and the cap has never been cut; the only cuts in the payroll tax occur passively when the income structure shifts so that a smaller fraction of AGI takes the form of wages and salaries under the cap, as happened in the late 1990s when the wage and salary share of adjusted gross income shrank, and a greater fraction of wages and salaries were over the cap. Why do payroll tax rates increase so much more easily than personal income tax rates? Perhaps partly due to a relative lack of resistance to the payroll tax, thanks to its greater efficiency per dollar collected.

Inefficient taxes seem to limit the growth of government. Perhaps it is no accident that the larger European governments have relied more heavily on relatively efficient, flat, and broad-based taxes like the payroll tax and VAT. Table 2, for the year 1995, shows how France, Germany, and the Netherlands each collected a greater fraction of their revenue from payroll taxes. Two of the four European countries had lower corporate income tax rates, and a third tied with the United States.

FIGURE 2
FEDERAL REVENUES FROM INDIVIDUAL INCOME AND SOCIAL SECURITY TAXES, 1946–2002 TAX YEARS

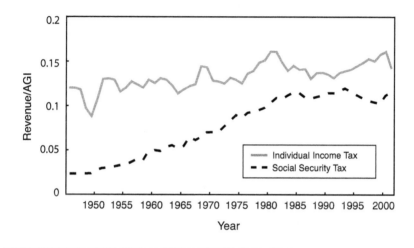

Source: Revenues from U.S. Office of Management and Budget (2005); AGI from IRS *Statistics of Income*, various issues.

What should we think about tax reform—in particular proposals to reduce the excess burden per dollar collected? A complete accounting of the costs and benefits of tax reform not only includes revenue but also recognizes the costs or benefits of the marginal public expenditure. If the marginal public expenditures have costs that sufficiently exceed their benefits, tax reform can increase the *total* excess burden, even while reducing the excess burden *per dollar collected*, by increasing total dollars collected. In this case, should we conclude, as Milton Friedman has said, that "the only good tax is a bad tax" (Barro 1997, 126)? Should the tax system be sabotaged, rather than improved?

The answer may be "no," for two reasons. First of all, not all excess burdens are created equal. For example, if we expect the marginal public expenditure to be financed with higher tax rates on labor income, then it will be the excess burden of labor-income taxes that stimulates taxpayer resistance to big government, and there is no reason to tolerate other excess burdens, such as those from capital-income taxation. Compliance

TABLE 2

THE INTERNATIONAL RELATION BETWEEN TAX MIX AND
TOTAL TAX REVENUE, 1995

Country	Payroll tax revenue (% of total revenue)	Corporate income tax rate (%)	All tax revenue (% of GDP)
France	43	33	45
Germany	39	45	39
Netherlands	42	35	44
United Kingdom	18	33	35
United States	25	35	28

SOURCE: Data for 1995 are from OECD (1998) and the American Council for Capital Formation (2001).
NOTE: Revenue statistic is for all levels of government; corporate tax rate for the central government only.

costs might also be reduced without stimulating government growth, if marginal public expenditures are to be financed with higher tax rates but not necessarily higher compliance costs. Yet another reason to discriminate among excess burdens is that some of them fall upon the politically weak and hence have little impact on the amount of public spending; reducing such burdens increases efficiency without expanding the budget.

Second, tax reform might be able to include cheaper ways of limiting public spending. In other words, maybe political reform needs to accompany tax reform.[6] Unfortunately, research in the field of political economy so far gives us little guidance as to what kinds of political reforms might help. Much of the theory focuses on details of the voting process, while empirical studies show that democratic and nondemocratic governments have quite similar budgets (Mulligan, Gil, and Sala-i-Martin 2004). A sizable empirical literature (surveyed by Besley and Case 2003) has documented cross-state correlations between political institutions and the amount of public spending. For example, states requiring a supermajority for raising tax rates seem to have less public spending; perhaps such a rule at the federal level would counterbalance the temptation to expand the public sector after the tax system had been made more efficient.

On the other hand, the cross-state data do not tell us whether supermajority rules limit spending, or whether citizens' demands for limited spending create the supermajority rules. Maybe this possibility is most obvious from the *positive* cross-state correlation between the amount of public spending and the existence of legislated caps on tax rates! Another problem with the cross-state data for our purposes is that, due to inter-state migration, an individual state faces much more competition for its citizens and businesses than does the federal government. There may exist political institutions that would successfully limit federal spending but not state spending, because the latter is already limited by migration. Until we have better knowledge of the effects of political institutions and how to combine tax reform with political reform, the problem may be part of the solution: Taxes' excess burden may be the most reliable restraint on public spending.

Notes

1. For details of these calculations, see Mulligan (2004) and the references cited therein.

2. The years surrounding the Kennedy tax cut are the major exception.

3. These law changes may have hurt capital market efficiency in other dimensions, without being revealed in figure 1, by adversely affecting the mix of capital goods. But the general point remains: Taxes affect efficiency.

4. It is also possible that government growth is resisted most when taxes are more "visible." This possibility is hard to distinguish empirically from my hypothesis, even though it has unique implications for the optimal design of a tax reform (see also Becker and Mulligan 2003).

5. It is feasible, in this example, for the persons with $50,000 in potential income to behave as if there were no taxes and have a liability of $10,000. Since they willingly reduce their income-earning effort in response to the tax, they must be better off than they would be paying $10,000 in taxes. Hence, in this example, the tax and excess burden must sum to less than $10,000 for persons with $50,000 potential income.

6. See also Mulligan and Sala-i-Martin (2004). A related motive for political reform is to prevent or at least delay the reformed tax system's evolving back to its prereform state.

References

American Council for Capital Formation. 2001. *The Role of Federal Tax Policy and Regulatory Reform in Promoting Economic Recovery and Long-Term Growth*. Washington, D.C.: American Council for Capital Formation. November.

Barro, Robert J. 1993. Retroactivity-Bungled Larceny. *Wall Street Journal*, August 17.

———. 1997. *Getting It Right: Markets and Choices in a Free Society*. Cambridge, Mass.: MIT Press.

Becker, Gary S., and Casey B. Mulligan. 2003. Deadweight Costs and the Size of Government. *Journal of Law and Economics* 46 (2): 293–340.

Besley, Timothy, and Anne Case. 2003. Political Institutions and Policy Choices: Evidence from the United States. *Journal of Economic Literature* 41 (March): 7–73.

European Commision. 2004. *VAT Rates Applied in the Member States of the European Community*. Brussels: European Commision. http://europa.eu.int/comm/taxation_customs/resources/documents/vat_rates_2004-en.pdf.

Fischer, Stanley, and Lawrence H. Summers. 1989. Should Governments Learn to Live with Inflation? *American Economic Review* 79 (2): 382–87.

Hall, Robert E., and Alvin Rabushka. 1995. *The Flat Tax*. 2nd ed. Stanford, Calif.: Hoover Institution Press.

Mulligan, Casey B. 2001. Economic Limits on "Rational" Democratic Redistribution. Working Paper No. 01.7, Harris School, University of Chicago, March.

———. 2004. What Do Aggregate Consumption Euler Equations Say about the Capital Income Tax Burden? *American Economic Review* 94 (2): 166–70.

Mulligan, Casey B., Ricard Gil, and Xavier Sala-i-Martin. 2004. Do Democracies Have Different Public Policies than Nondemocracies? *Journal of Economic Perspectives* 18 (1): 51–74.

Mulligan, Casey B., and Xavier Sala-i-Martin. 2004. Political and Economic Forces Sustaining Social Security. *Advances in Economic Analysis & Policy* 4 (1): Article 5.

Organisation for Economic Co-operation and Development. 1998. *Revenue Statistics of OECD Member Countries*. Paris: OECD.

———. 2004. *OECD in Figures*. Paris: OECD.

Slemrod, Joel. 1998. Methodological Issues in Measuring and Interpreting Taxable Income Elasticities. *National Tax Journal* 51 (4): 773–88.

U.S. Department of the Treasury. Internal Revenue Service. *Statistics of Income*. Various issues.

U.S. Office of Management and Budget. 2005. *Historical Tables, Budget of the United States Government, Fiscal Year 2005*. Washington, D.C.: U.S. Government Printing Office.

U.S. Social Security Administration. 2004. *Social Security Programs throughout the World*. Washington, D.C.: U.S. Government Printing Office.

7

A Tax Reform Caveat: In the Real World, There Is No Perfect Tax System

Ronald A. Pearlman

> *Every tax system has Achilles' heels. Theorists advocate simplicity; reality produces complexity. On Sunday morning, our national leaders speak of fairness; during the workweek, the legislative process yields inequality. Economists preach efficiency; interest groups advocate special treatment. Moreover, in the real world, every tax system is vulnerable to tax avoidance and tax evasion, much of it unanticipated during the legislative process.*
> —Ronald A. Pearlman (1998, 569)

I made this statement several years ago in discussing fundamental tax reform. It reflects skepticism with what I consider to be overly optimistic promises of reform. Present law has problems. It is distortive. It bears the appearance of unfairness among individual taxpayers with different income sources and among business taxpayers in different sectors of the economy. And it is complex for business taxpayers and millions of individual taxpayers. However, as we embark on another national tax reform debate, it is well to bear in mind that individual and corporate income taxes account for nearly one trillion dollars in revenues, even after the substantial tax reductions over the past several years, and represent slightly over 87 percent of government receipts if social insurance taxes are disregarded (U.S. Executive Office of the President, Office of Management and Budget 2005). It also is worth remembering that Americans enjoy the most vibrant economy in the world—in spite of what some believe to be a deficient tax system. And, finally, although discussion of pure tax-reform options is interesting and intellectually challenging, we live in the real world.

As we approach the twentieth anniversary of the Tax Reform Act of 1986, the last comprehensive examination of the federal income tax, it is appropriate to consider ways to improve the tax system, whether by moving to an idealized income tax, replacing the current tax with a consumption tax, or making substantial refinements to the existing hybrid tax system. However, travel from a theoretical discussion of tax-reform options to enacted legislation will be along a largely uncharted and bumpy road. Thus, this essay reflects my view that we should approach significant changes to the tax law with considerable caution.

I am a lawyer, not an economist. Even though presently I am a teacher, I was not trained as an academic and do not consider myself a scholar. Rather, my views about tax reform are informed primarily by twenty-eight years as a practicing tax lawyer, representing real people in real-life situations, and three forays into government, including six years in tax policy positions at the Treasury Department and the Joint Committee on Taxation. I believe a pragmatic rather than an idealistic approach to tax reform is desirable as a matter of tax policy and is most realistic legislatively.

It may seem strange to waste an opportunity in this essay to advocate an idealized tax regime. However, I do not consider it a waste. I am ambivalent about the desirability of implementing any "pure" alternative to present law, even if it were politically possible. Two things are certain. First, change is traumatic and unpredictable. Radical proposals present unanswerable questions. No group of experts can accurately predict the inevitable fiscal, economic, social, compliance, and other effects that would accompany a dramatic change in the tax law, such as a wholesale rejection of our current tax system. Second, legislation resulting from an attempt to enact an ideal tax will not be pure. The United States can ill afford to risk the current predictable revenue stream generated by the income tax or the unpredictable behavioral responses to an entirely new tax system. Moreover, if our political leaders are up to the task, proposals to reform the current system can be bold and constructive.

My discussion of tax reform is divided into two parts. Following a very brief comment about present law, I make some observations about the possibility of adopting a pure income tax or one of several pure consumption taxes. I then offer some selected proposals intended to improve and rationalize the current hybrid tax system.

The Present System and the Implications of Change

I do not share the views of some that the present hybrid income tax is fundamentally flawed and beyond repair. A tax system that raises the amount of revenue generated currently while apparently not inflicting undue damage on a generally robust economy cannot be all that bad. Nevertheless, I recognize that some believe it desirable to adopt a pure form of taxation, either an idealized income tax or, more likely, an idealized consumption tax. For several reasons, I do not share that view.

A Pure Income Tax. An income tax that adheres to the Haig-Simons model would accurately measure and evenly tax the economic income of individuals and businesses (Haig 1921, Simons 1938). It would tax business income once, but only once, and it would omit most of the exclusions, deductions, and credits presently available to individuals and businesses, notwithstanding their social desirability or perceived incentive effects. It also would not provide reduced tax rates for particular types of income, such as long-term capital gains, qualified dividend income, or other income from capital.

As a practical matter, however, we are unable to implement a pure income tax because we cannot accurately measure economic income. I offer two among many examples. First, experience suggests that it would be impossible to determine the taxable personal-consumption component of numerous noncash elements of an employment relationship, such as an employer-provided corner office, cell phone, or trip to a business meeting in a warm climate. Second, it would be impossible to design an empirically perfect system of economic depreciation, that is, one which properly reflects the precise economic life and rate of decline in the productivity of every category of business asset.

Other important practical problems preclude implementation of a pure income tax. For example, it is unlikely that Congress would override the realization principle, one of the major departures in current law from an idealized income, even though I think the U.S. income tax system could tolerate a mark-to-market accrual system limited to readily marketable assets. We also must not ignore the complexity and administrability of a tax system designed to measure accurately all economic income. The Treasury Department's 1984 tax reform report to the president represented an effort to measure economic income more accurately (U.S. Department of the Treasury 1984). In my opinion, it contained many constructive proposals. However, as detractors correctly observe, moving to a more idealized income tax inevitably results in increased complexity. Consider, for example, the difficulty of designing and implementing provisions that index, first, investment gains that are not subject to a mark-to-market regime, to ensure that only real and not inflationary gains are subject to tax; second, the basis of depreciable assets, to ensure that depreciation deductions reflect the inflation in the cost of business property; and third, debt, in order to measure deductible interest expense and includable interest income accurately.

Full-Replacement Option. Even if it were possible to adopt and implement a pure income tax, many tax policy analysts point out that an income tax is not neutral with respect to the choice between saving and current consumption. They maintain that the resulting distortion impedes economic growth and, therefore, the United States should reject the income tax entirely in favor of a consumption-based tax, or "full-replacement option."

Critics are correct in asserting that a pure income tax imposes a heavier burden on savings than on current consumption. Nevertheless, I believe there are at least six reasons for rejecting a full replacement of the income tax with a consumption-based tax.

The first reason relates to fairness, both actual and perceived. An appropriately designed income tax, that is, one that evenly, even if imprecisely, taxes all economic income, serves to measure broadly individuals' relative abilities to pay tax and, thereby, share the cost of government, and it does so in a transparent manner that most people understand. Simply stated, I think Americans instinctively relate income-earning capacity to the fairness of the tax system. Thus, a decision to reject economic income as an appropriate measuring rod raises two important questions. First, is it possible that a consumption-tax replacement will, in fact, change the present distribution of the tax burden in a way that makes the tax law less progressive? Second, will Americans perceive a tax system that is not based on income to be less fair?

Proponents generally acknowledge that a consumption tax will fall more heavily on individuals who spend a relatively larger share of their earnings and assets on basic consumption, such as clothing, food, and housing.[1] I realize that it is possible to build some progressivity into a consumption tax as do Professor David Bradford's "X tax" and the Hall-Rabushka flat tax, a subtraction-method value-added tax (Bradford 2004, 2; Hall and Rabushka 1995). It also would be possible to create a new direct-payment program to soften the regressivity of a pure consumption tax.

As a noneconomist, I do not fully understand and, thus, tend to pay less attention to theoretical economic models. Perhaps as a result, I am skeptical that any tax system that exempts income from capital from tax at the individual level—the central feature of every consumption tax— will replicate the distribution of the current tax system, even after the consumption tax is fully phased in many years in the future. And, even if the distribution may be replicated as a matter of theory, exempting income from capital from tax creates the likelihood that Americans will view the tax system as disproportionately favoring the most well-off members of society. As Dr. Richard Land, president of the Ethics and Religious Liberty Commission of the Southern Baptist Convention, recently stated, "People are not going to give the kind of support necessary for tax reform that leaves the investor class untaxed. That is not going to be politically viable" (Andrews and Kirkpatrick 2004).

At the most general level, tax reform may be perceived as simply presenting the question whether the law should move in the direction of a strengthened income tax, whether a consumption-based tax should be adopted in its place, or whether our present hybrid system should be retained in some form. However, it is impossible to answer this broad question without first determining whether and to what extent income from capital should be subject to, or exempt from, tax. Thus, the taxation of income from capital becomes the central tax policy issue facing policymakers in the current tax reform debate.

My second reason for rejecting a full replacement option relates to transition. As I have suggested elsewhere, it would be unfair and politically impossible to refuse to ameliorate the abrupt shift from an income tax to a pure consumption tax without meaningful transitional relief (Pearlman 1996, 393; a sequel to this paper is Pearlman 1997, 17). Imagine the reaction of a business taxpayer who has made significant pre-change investments in business assets when the taxpayer discovers that the business will not be entitled to depreciate or otherwise recover the cost of these investments following the repeal of the present income tax and enactment of a new consumption tax. The owners of that business may be expected to demand appropriate transition relief, and members of Congress will sympathetically respond. Thus, transition to a consumption tax would be very costly. It would reduce, and perhaps even eliminate, the one-time economic benefit of moving to a consumption tax.

Third, implementation of a consumption tax does not ensure the simplification and improved tax compliance advocated by some proponents. A cash-flow consumption tax presents important definitional and measurement issues, and European-style value-added tax (VAT) systems have long been vulnerable to fraud and evasion.[2]

Fourth, the primary goal of any tax system should be to raise the revenues necessary to finance government. As I indicated at the beginning of this essay, if we exclude social insurance programs, the corporate and individual income taxes account for virtually all of the federal government's receipts. Most tax revenues are collected efficiently as a result of an effective wage-withholding system and a relatively high level of voluntary compliance. Replacement of the income tax with a consumption tax carries with it the risk that implementation and unanticipated avoidance and evasion will reduce government receipts. Assuming tax reform is to be revenue neutral, full replacement presents a potential fiscal risk.

Fifth, I am not persuaded that in a world in which every developed country has an income tax as part of its mix of national revenues, the United States should abandon the income tax entirely. It is worth asking, for example, whether our trading partners would be willing to enter into tax treaties with the United States in which they are asked to make income tax concessions while we, in the absence of an income tax, do not. The United States should strive to be a global tax-policy leader, but it should not wholly disregard international tax norms.

Finally, it is naïve to assume that it would be possible to enact an idealized consumption tax. Just as with the present income tax, enacted legislation will include important departures from a theoretically pure model. Should a retail sales tax or a credit-invoice method value-added tax replace the present income tax, the departures likely would take the form of multiple tax rates or exemptions for, among other things, housing, certain services, and selected pharmaceuticals and food products. If the replacement were a subtraction-method VAT or expenditure tax, we might expect the law to include special deductions and exemptions. Whatever the form of a replacement option, it would be full of exceptions from a theoretically pure model. To paraphrase the movie *Field of Dreams*, if you enact it, they will come.

A Hybrid Tax System. Even though we refer to the principal federal tax as an income tax, it is not a pure income tax but, rather, a hybrid system that contains both income- and consumption-tax elements.[3] A hybrid tax presents its own set of problems and, thus, is not ideal. Nevertheless, because of the inability to adopt and implement either a pure income tax or a pure consumption tax, I favor taking steps to substantially improve the hybrid system.

Continuation of a hybrid tax system accommodates the "ability to pay" feature of the income tax and the asserted capital formation benefits of a consumption tax. This approach reasonably ensures a stable future revenue stream without the risks of a full-replacement option. Moreover, it also should be possible to meaningfully simplify compliance for individuals and business taxpayers.

To proponents of an income tax who are concerned about the regressivity and potential unfairness of consumption-tax elements in a hybrid system, I offer two observations. First, as I attempted to illustrate, a pure income tax is an unrealistic model. Second, it is not clear in a global economy that, on the long term, income from capital may comprehensively be subjected to tax. To the extent that businesses based in the United States derive increasing amounts of income abroad and locate increasing amounts of their intellectual property in foreign jurisdictions, one must question the ability of the United States to successfully collect tax on the income attributable to these foreign activities. Moreover, to the extent U.S. businesses are taxed more heavily than foreign competitors, it is likely that investment capital will gravitate to business activity not subject to tax in the United States.

Even at the individual level, the future taxation of income from capital is problematic. A global financial system makes it relatively easy for individual taxpayers to locate financial assets in foreign jurisdictions. These investors may increasingly choose not to report foreign-earned investment income in their U.S. tax returns. Without a worldwide exchange of information and a tax enforcement network among all relevant governments, detection of such omitted income by the tax collector of any one country, including the United States, is difficult. Thus, even if one accepts the merits of including income from capital in the tax base—a fundamental characteristic of an income tax—it is important to realize the practical limitations on the future ability of any single government to do so.

Practical Reforms of a Hybrid System

During the Treasury Department's consideration of tax-reform options leading to the Tax Reform Act of 1986, we coupled proposals to broaden the individual- and business-tax bases with meaningful reductions in income tax rates. The combination of base broadening and rate reduction reduces the economic distortions that result from high tax rates and sector-specific tax incentives and increases the perception that the tax system applies fairly to everyone.

I favor a renewed effort to combine base broadening with rate reduction. The present alternative minimum tax (AMT) is defective—primarily, in my opinion, because of the rate structure, the fact that it does not allow taxpayers to receive the benefit of personal exemptions, and the fact that it does not allow the deduction of miscellaneous itemized deductions even with respect to expenses directly related to the production of business or investment income. However, a reformed AMT could serve as a model for a base-broadened income tax. In considering this possibility, it is relevant that approximately 50 percent of the revenue raised by the current individual AMT is attributable to the disallowance of the deduction of state and local income taxes in calculating alternative minimum taxable income. If repeal of the regular tax deduction for state and local income taxes is considered a viable tax-reform option, it is noteworthy that the present AMT already achieves this result.

Without underestimating the power of special interests, policymakers should explore bold modifications of the individual tax base that would exclude at least some current itemized deductions, statutory exclusions from income, and individual tax credits. If the resulting tax revenues are used to reduce individual income-tax rates, at some point people might conclude that a lower tax rate is an appropriate tradeoff for giving up various targeted provisions of current law. Indeed, if one favors replacing the income tax with a consumption tax, this might be an attractive option.

Recognizing the Utopian nature of this proposal, it nevertheless would be productive to determine how far a base-broadening/rate-reduction approach might successfully be pursued. Presumably, some of the sacred cows, such as the home-mortgage interest and charitable-contribution deductions, will not be repealed in their entirety. However, it might be possible to scale them back, for example, by reducing the present million-dollar cap on the home mortgage interest deduction to $250,000 or $500,000 and either repealing the deduction for interest on home equity indebtedness or lowering the present $100,000 cap to $25,000 or $50,000. Similarly, it might be possible to limit the deductibility of charitable contributions of appreciated property to the lower of the fair-market value or adjusted-tax basis of such property. There is no principled tax-policy rationale that justifies the deduction of an amount equal to the appreciation in the value of tangible or real property that has not been included in the donor's income.

I favor repeal of the 2 percent floor on miscellaneous itemized deductions and the 3 percent limit on itemized deductions (the so-called Pease limitation). In 1984, I was persuaded by members of the Treasury staff of the merits of the 2 percent floor. My instincts at the time suggested that it was inappropriate to deny even a small part of a deduction for an expense relating to the earning or production of income, but I was attracted to the simplification possibilities and the recognition that some deductible expenses, such as subscriptions to popular business publications, include a personal consumption element. However, experience since the enactment of the 1986 act confirms my instincts. The 2 percent floor improperly restricts the deduction of legitimate and, in some cases, substantial business-related expenses.

I was on the staff of the Joint Committee on Taxation when the Pease limitation was enacted in 1990. At the time, everyone knew that the limitation was a backdoor tax-rate increase. However, an explicit rate increase was not politically possible, and subsequent recommendations to replace the Pease limitation with a revenue-neutral offsetting rate increase have been rejected. If we are to reform the present system, truth-in-advertising demands permanent repeal of the Pease limitation.

In addition to these suggestions, I offer what I consider to be three bold reform proposals. The first relates to the design of a tax-favored, nonretirement savings vehicle, the second to the tax treatment of debt, and the third to simplified tax reporting.

The president has proposed the adoption of a so-called "lifetime savings account," a tax-favored, nonretirement savings vehicle. The existence of various tax-sheltered savings vehicles in present law, including retirement savings incentives, contributes to its characterization as a hybrid tax system. If the tax system is to be used to encourage savings, a policy decision that I would condition on a convincing demonstration that any savings incentive will increase savings at the margin, then the law should be market neutral. Under present law, savings incentives are not market neutral. New legislation that layers a new tax-sheltered savings vehicle on top of those currently permitted will not result in neutrality. Today, it is possible to shelter savings that are not intended to be used for retirement in at least two ways, first, by purchasing a whole-life insurance policy and, second, by investing in a so-called deferred annuity. In either case, because of the tax deferral accorded the inside buildup in the contract, the earnings on investments accrue tax-free until withdrawn by the contract owner. As a practical matter, there is no limitation on the amount of assets that may be used to fund a whole-life insurance policy or a deferred annuity, or on the amount of income that may be sheltered. As a result, these two insurance products have a competitive edge over all forms of taxable savings, such as bank and brokerage accounts and mutual funds.[4]

There is no reason one form of investment should be favored over another. If an individual prefers to invest by means of a stock brokerage account, why should income and gains be subject to current tax at the same time her neighbor invests the same amount of funds in a deferred annuity? I assume that consumption-tax advocates would tend to favor eliminating situations where the tax system creates economic distortion. Since it is likely that enhanced tax-favored savings will be a part of a tax-reform effort, this would be an ideal time to remove a troublesome distortion in current law. To do so, it is not necessary to preclude investors from using life insurance or annuity products. Rather, the availability of tax deferral when utilizing such investments should be subject to the same limitations applicable to any newly enacted tax-sheltered savings vehicle. For example, if the president proposes a new $100,000 tax-sheltered savings account, then an individual should be able to establish the account as an annuity or whole-life insurance policy or as an appropriately identified bank, brokerage, or other investment account. Income on amounts that a taxpayer invests in excess of the $100,000 statutory maximum should be taxed currently, no matter how invested. Likewise, rules relating to the deductibility or nondeductibility of contributions, the tax treatment of distributions, and any restrictions and penalties on impermissible withdrawals should apply to all tax-sheltered investment options.

Of course, the insurance industry will not be happy with my proposal. However, tax reform is intended to be bold. If tax reform were to result in a single set of rules being applied to all tax-sheltered savings vehicles, every financial product would be required to compete in the marketplace on its own merits, based on its nontax characteristics. Moreover, the base-broadening effect of constraining the present unlimited use of annuities and life insurance would enable Congress to use the additional revenues to liberalize the maximum-dollar limit or other restrictions on the permitted tax-sheltered account.

The second proposed change to existing law relates to the tax treatment of debt. Allowing a taxpayer to deduct interest expense at the same time income from capital is either explicitly or effectively exempt from tax does not increase net savings. Moreover, it is more generous than the treatment of debt in a pure consumption tax, may result in negative tax rates whereby the government is paying part of the cost of the investment and, inevitably, will result in tax avoidance through the creation of tax shelters. Under present law, notwithstanding some limited legislative efforts to the contrary, this is the current state of play. If tax reform results in the expansion of tax-sheltered savings opportunities, the arbitrage possibilities of present law will increase. In my opinion, this possibility is very trouble-some and should be considered unacceptable by policymakers.

I propose a strict limitation, utilizing a mechanical-apportionment rule, on the deductibility by individuals of any otherwise deductible interest expense whenever an individual invests some or all of her capital in a form that yields explicit or implicit tax-exempt income. Money is fungible. Therefore, disallowance of the deduction for interest expense should not be limited to debt directly traceable to the assets that yield the tax-exempt return. If an individual invests in a tax-sheltered savings vehi-cle, including tax-deferred annuities and life insurance, in which the real-ization of investment income is deferred and reinvested tax-free, some portion of the individual's interest expense should be denied, without regard to whether the debt is traceable to the tax-sheltered investment, and even if the interest expense otherwise is deductible as investment interest or home mortgage interest.

As with the individual income tax, tax reform also must include a bold reexamination of the business tax base. I am particularly interested in various provisions of current law that allow the partial or full expens-ing of the cost of business assets and provisions that materially accelerate depreciation or amortization deductions. On the surface, these provisions appear merely to improve a business taxpayer's cash flow in the year the cost of the asset is deducted. However, analysts have long known that expensing is the present-value equivalent of exempting income from the asset from future tax. Even if expensing is considered an acceptable norm, policymakers must understand this present-value effect. If, on reflection, a closer matching of business income and expenses is deemed appropri-ate, as I believe to be the case, then revenues resulting from a more con-servative cost-recovery regime could be used to reduce tax rates on all business income, including the income of service businesses that are not heavily reliant on investments in machinery and equipment, thereby making the tax system more neutral and, therefore, more efficient.

Related to a review of the cost-recovery rules of present law, we should reexamine the extent to which a business taxpayer is entitled to deduct interest expense. For the reasons noted above in discussing indi-vidual tax-sheltered investments, it is very important that the deductibil-ity of interest expense should be restricted in the case of those business taxpayers whose income from assets is fully or partially exempt from tax on a present-value basis because of liberal cost-recovery rules.

There are numerous other business-tax provisions issues that might be considered as part of the current tax-reform discussion. For example, I think it would be instructive to review the various forms of doing business, including the multiple pass-through structures of existing law; the taxation of foreign income; the double taxation of at least some corporate earnings; and the exemption of investment income earned by tax-exempt and foreign investors.

My third and final proposal relates to individual tax simplification. Although tax simplification means different things to different categories of taxpayers, tax compliance clearly is more burdensome than it need be for millions of individual taxpayers. The Treasury Department's 1984 tax-reform recommendations included a so-called return-free proposal whereby at least some individual taxpayers would not be required to file a tax return (U.S. Department of the Treasury 1984). Unfortunately, in the process of finalizing the 1984 document, we ran out of the time necessary to develop the proposal fully, and, frankly, we ran into some resistance within the bureaucracy.

I continue to believe it is possible to provide meaningful compliance assistance to a large number of individual taxpayers by easing for them the burden of preparing tax returns without totally divorcing them from the income tax or the return filing process. The key is to place the primary responsibility for preparing tax returns on the IRS or federally financed contractors and thereby relieve individual taxpayers of the burden and cost of preparing their own tax returns.

Even under current law, it would be possible in many cases for the IRS to prepare an individual's tax return based on information obtained from third parties and very minor input from the taxpayer. In more complicated situations, where the tax return must contain added information known only to the taxpayer, for example, information that relates to eligibility for the Earned Income Tax Credit or other tax benefits under current law, a new, simplified return system would allow taxpayers to provide the necessary factual information to the IRS, which then would use the information to prepare the individual's return. Similarly, if withholding on income at source is not always possible, as would, for example, likely be the case for certain payments to independent contractors, then the simplified system would allow the taxpayer to provide the IRS with information regarding any additional income and, following preparation of the individual's tax return by the IRS, require the individual to make an additional tax payment.

Characterization of a simplified tax return preparation system as "return-free" is misleading. In order for the taxpayer to understand the manner in which her tax liability was calculated and appreciate her contribution to the cost of government, it is desirable for the taxpayer to examine and review her return. However, the return preparation process should be free and as painless as reasonably possible. If the president were to advocate, and Congress were to adopt, a simplified return system, taxpayers would hail the action as an historic simplification of the tax law.

Conclusion

I hope the impending discussion of tax reform will result in constructive changes to the federal tax system. However, I have reservations about the environment in which the debate will occur. There are fundamental disagreements between advocates of a full-replacement option and those who support continuation of the income tax. Indeed, there are disagreements among full-replacement advocates regarding the proper form of a consumption tax. We are a long way from a national consensus on the proper direction of fundamental tax reform. I fear that the inevitable political compromises in such an environment—for example, enactment of enhanced tax-sheltered savings incentives or expensing of capital investments without any further limitations on the deductibility of interest expense—may lead to an erosion of tax revenues and a reduction in the tax burden on those individuals most able to bear the costs of government.

I also fear that criticisms of the Internal Revenue Service, popular with politicians at least since President Carter, will creep into the tax reform debate. Unfair criticism of the tax collector, including unrealistic proposals to eliminate the IRS, will further erode IRS employee morale and Americans' confidence in the tax system. The president and members of Congress would do well to stick to the consideration of, and debate on, ways to improve the tax system and avoid unjustifiably making the IRS the scapegoat for perceived imperfections in current law.

It is relatively easy to generalize about fundamental tax reform: Simplify the law, make it fair, and stimulate economic growth. It is much more difficult to enter the trenches to design specific provisions, attempt to determine the winners and losers, predict how proposed law changes likely will be interpreted and what avoidance and evasion potentials exist, and establish whether specific proposals will be administrable. Discussion of tax reform understandably is general at present. However, it is important for policymakers to remember that in order to achieve broad tax policy objectives, it is best not to leave design and implementation issues until the end. Otherwise, we might find that what has been promised cannot be delivered.

Notes

1. Some tax-reform advocates reject progressivity as a desirable goal. However, I doubt this view is widely held and, therefore, think it would not be reflected in a major reform of the income tax.

2. "It is difficult to get an accurate picture, but it is clear from the few studies that have been published that VAT evasion is widespread and involves significant revenue losses, though the extent varies considerably across countries" (Webley, Adams, and Elffers 2002, 1).

3. Indeed, in at least one respect, the present system is worse than a pure consumption tax because it allows the deductibility of interest expense even though the taxpayer enjoys exemption or deferral from tax-sheltered savings, expensing, and other assorted business-tax incentives.

4. In the interest of full disclosure, I note that I serve as an independent trustee of a family of mutual funds.

References

Andrews, Edmund L., and David D. Kirkpatrick. 2004. G.O.P. Constituencies Split on Tax Change. *New York Times*. November 22, C1.

Bradford, David F. 2004. *The X Tax in the World Economy: Going Global with a Simple, Progressive Tax*. Washington, D.C.: AEI Press.

Haig, Robert M, ed. 1921. *The Federal Income Tax*, chapter 1. New York: Columbia University Press.

Hall, Robert E., and Alvin Rabushka. 1995. *The Flat Tax*, 2nd ed. Stanford, Calif.: Hoover Institution Press.

Pearlman, Ronald A. 1996. Transition Issues in Moving to a Consumption Tax: A Tax Lawyer's Perspective. In Henry J. Aaron and William G. Gale, eds. *Economic Effects of Fundamental Tax Reform*. Washington, D.C.: Brookings Institution Press.

———. 1997. Transition Issues in Moving to a Consumption Tax. In *A Comprehensive Analysis of Current Consumption Tax Proposals*. Chicago: American Bar Association.

———. 1998. Fresh from the River Styx: The Achilles' Heels of Tax Reform Proposals. *National Tax Journal* 51:569.

Simons, Henry C. 1938. *Personal Income Taxation*. Chicago: University of Chicago Press.

U.S. Department of the Treasury. 1984. *Tax Reform for Fairness, Simplicity, and Economic Growth: The Treasury Department Report to the President*. U.S. Department of the Treasury, November.

U.S. Executive Office of the President. Office of Management and Budget. 2005. *Budget of the United States Government*. Analytical Perspectives, Federal Receipts, table 17-1. Receipts by Source, FY 2006, p. 263. www.whitehouse. gov/omb/budget/fy2006/pdf/spec.pdf (accessed March 29, 2005).

Webley, Paul, Caroline Adams, and Henk Elffers. 2002. VAT Compliance in the United Kingdom. Working Paper 41. Canberra, Australia: Centre for Tax System Integrity, Research School of Social Sciences, Australian National University. December. http://ctsi.anu.edu.au/publications/WP/41.pdf (accessed March 29, 2005).

8

The Elasticity of Labor Supply and the Consequences for Tax Policy

Edward C. Prescott

There is an old maxim which states that good judgment comes from experience, and experience comes from poor judgment. I think something similar can be said of government policy, to wit: Good policy comes from experience, and experience comes from poor policy.

This bit of homespun wisdom could easily apply to all sorts of government policies over time, but it has particular relevance to tax policy and, specifically, to the U.S. Social Security system. Created during the Great Depression to guarantee that no senior citizen should live in poverty, Social Security was a good idea meant to address the growing needs of elderly Americans. However, good ideas don't always equal good policy.

Social Security was developed at a time when the number of workers paying into the system greatly outnumbered those who were receiving funds, and thus the promise made by government was easily kept. But times change while policies atrophy, and Social Security has evolved into a system that places an increasing burden on the young: The ratio of workers to Social Security beneficiaries has shifted from about forty-one to one in the 1930s to roughly three to one today.

Young workers today are being told that their Social Security contributions—or taxes—may have to increase to support the burgeoning elderly population. Moreover, those young workers are being warned that the same benefits will not apply to them—that they will have to work longer and receive less than the folks they are now supporting. Such are government promises, especially those grounded on ill-founded policy.

Poor policies, though, need not persist. We really can learn from experience, and we should apply that experience and new knowledge to existing policies so those original good ideas—and government promises—can be made whole. Regarding tax policy, we have learned that labor supply is not inelastic and does, indeed, respond to changes in tax rates. This insight, so simple and yet so powerful, has implications for all sorts of tax policies, and one that would greatly benefit from its application is the U.S. Social Security tax system. This chapter will discuss the impact of tax rates on labor supply and the implications for U.S. tax policy. If labor supply elasticities are high, then getting tax reform wrong can have terrible economic effects. I will focus on the damage done by Social Security as a special case, but the conclusions suggest that tax reforms that broaden the base and reduce marginal rates have tremendous promise.

Labor Supply Responds to Tax Rates

Let's begin by considering a commonly held view which says that labor supply is not affected by tax rates. In other words, this idea holds that hours worked in the market will remain steady when tax rates are either raised or lowered. If you are a policymaker and you subscribe to this view, then you can confidently increase marginal tax rates as high as you like to attain the revenues you desire. Not only that, but you can move those tax rates up and down whenever you like and blithely assume that this will have no effect on output. This is what economists and policymakers used to believe; unfortunately, many still do.

However, economic theory and data have come together to prove this notion wrong, and we have many different laboratories—or countries—in which we can view live experiments. The most useful comparison is between the United States and the countries of Europe because these economies share similar traits, but the data also hold when we consider other countries.

This issue is encapsulated in one question that is currently puzzling policymakers: Why do Americans work so much more than Europeans? The answer to this question is important because it suggests policy proposals that will improve European standards of living. However, an incorrect answer will result in policies that will only exacerbate Europe's problems and could have implications for other countries that are looking for best practices.

Here is a somewhat startling fact: Based on labor-market statistics from the Organisation for Economic Co-operation and Development (OECD), Americans aged fifteen to sixty-four, on a per-person basis, work 50 percent more than do the French (Prescott 2004). Comparisons between Americans and Germans or Italians are similar. What's going on here? What can possibly account for these large differences in labor supply?

It turns out the answer is not related to cultural differences or institutional factors like unemployment benefits; rather, marginal tax rates explain virtually all of this difference. I admit that when I first conducted this analysis I was surprised by this finding, because I fully expected institutional constraints to be playing a bigger role. But this is not the case.

Let's take another look at the data. According to the OECD, from 1970 to 1974 France's labor supply exceeded that of the United States. A review of other industrialized countries shows that their labor supplies also either exceeded or were comparable to the U.S. labor supply during this period. Jump ahead two decades, and you will find that France's labor supply dropped significantly (as did others), and that some countries improved and stayed in line with the United States. Controlling for other factors, what stands out in these cross-country comparisons is that when tax rates of European countries and the United States were comparable, their labor supplies were comparable (Prescott 2004).

And this insight does not apply just to Western industrialized economies. A review of Japanese and Chilean data reveals the same result (Hayashi and Prescott 2002; Bergoeing et al. 2002). This is an important point because some critics of this analysis have suggested that cultural differences explain the difference between European and American labor supplies. It is suggested that the French, for example, prefer leisure more than Americans do, or, on the other side of the coin, that Americans like to work more. This is silliness.

Again, I would point to the data which show that when the French and others were taxed at rates similar to Americans, they supplied roughly the same amount of labor. Other research has shown that at the aggregate level, where idiosyncratic preference differences are averaged out, people are remarkably similar across countries. Further, a recent study has shown that Germans and Americans spend the same amount of time working, but the proportion of taxable market time versus nontaxable home work time is different (Schettkat 2003). In other words, Germans work just as much, but more of their work is not captured in the taxable market.

I would add additional data for certain countries, especially Italy, that measure nontaxable market time, or the underground economy. Many Italians, for example, aren't necessarily working any less than Americans—they simply are not being taxed for some of their labor. Indeed, the Italian government increases its measured output by nearly 25 percent to capture the output of the underground sector. Change the tax laws, and you will notice a change in behavior: People won't start working more; they will simply engage in more taxable market labor and will produce more per hour worked.

This analysis has important implications for policy—not just for Europe, but for the United States as well. For example, much was made during the 2004 U.S. election season about whether the current administration's tax cuts were good or bad for the economy, but that misses the point. The real issue is whether it is better to tweak the economy with short-lived stimulus plans or to establish an efficient tax system with low tax rates that do not change with the political climate.

What does this mean for U.S. tax policy? It means that we should stop focusing on the recent tax cuts and, instead, start thinking about tax rates. And that means that we should roll back the 1993 tax-rate increases and reestablish those from the 1986 Tax Reform Act. Just as they did in the late 1980s, and just as they would in Europe, these lower rates would increase the labor supply, output would grow, and tax revenues would increase.

Now, might there be a small increase in debt as we move to a better tax system? Sure, but remember that the most important measure of debt is privately owned government debt as a percentage of gross national income, which has been flat over the past three years. Also, a surefire way to handle this increase in debt would be to cut expenditures. Actually, another way to handle it would be to pray to the gods for another high-tech boom. The debt would go "poof," and we'd praise whoever is president for being fiscally responsible.

Some say that the 1993 tax-rate hike was responsible for erasing this country's debt problems because it increased government revenues. This is false. The ratio of U.S. debt to gross national income continued to increase in the years following those rate hikes and did not fall until the fortuitous boom that occurred in the late 1990s. The high-tech boom meant that people worked more, output increased, incomes climbed, and tax revenues followed suit. You cannot tax your way to that sort of prosperity. Imagine the outcome of the late-1990s boom if tax rates had been lower.

And, by the way, lower tax rates are good for all taxpayers. We're barking up the wrong tree if we think that "taxing the rich" will solve all our problems. You know who these rich people are? They are often families with two professional wage-earners. If you tax that family too much, one wage-earner will drop out. That's bad not only for the income of that family but also for the output of the whole economy—and it will result in lower tax revenues.

Also, we need to get away from thinking of the rich as some sort of permanent class. Many of the individuals who show up on annual millionaire lists, for example, are people who happened to have had a good year and who may never appear on those lists again. Consider people who worked hard for many years and built a successful business that finally goes public. The big capital gain they realize that year is really compensation for the uncompensated effort they put into building the business. They should not be penalized for their vision and tenacity. If we establish rules that punish the winners, entrepreneurs will take fewer risks, and we will have less innovation, less output, and less job growth. The whole economy suffers under such a scenario—not just those few individuals who are taxed at a higher rate. And this doesn't just involve the Googles and Apples and Microsofts, but countless other companies that start small and end up making large contributions to the economy.

The important thing to remember is that the labor supply is not fixed. People, be they European or American, respond to taxes on their income. Just one more example: In 1998, Spain flattened its tax rates in similar fashion to the U.S. rate cuts of 1986, and the Spanish labor supply increased by 12 percent. In addition, Spanish tax revenues also increased by a few percent.

The bottom line is that a thorough analysis of historical data in the United States and Europe indicates that, given similar incentives, people make similar choices about labor and leisure. Free European workers from their tax bondage, and you will see an increase in gross domestic product. The same holds true for Americans.

Fixing Social Security by Fixing Tax Rates

The same also holds for the U.S. Social Security system. Remember those three young workers who have to support that one senior citizen? And remember how some policymakers want to raise taxes on those young workers, and how they also want to reduce their retirement benefits even as they work to provide more benefits to current retirees? Would such changes in tax rates and in government promises affect labor supply? Theory says yes, the statistical evidence agrees, and common sense concurs. These young workers are rational. They make labor/leisure choices on the margin, and these marginal choices add up.

So what to do? How do we move from a pay-as-you-go welfare system to a self-funding retirement system that benefits from individual profit-maximizing incentives? Again, the answer begins with the insight that labor supply is responsive to tax rates. We simply cannot keep cranking up Social Security taxes with impunity. We need to turn the present tax-and-transfer system into a bona fide individual retirement system that is in line with individual incentives.

In short, the answer is to establish a system of mandatory savings accounts for retirement. Why mandatory accounts? Because without them we will not solve the time-inconsistency problem of people undersaving and becoming a welfare burden on their families and on the taxpayers. That's exactly where we are now.

Before I describe the benefits of such accounts, let's begin by dismissing the notion that individual savings plans are somehow dangerous to U.S. citizens. Some politicians have vilified the idea of giving investment freedom to citizens, arguing that those citizens will be exposed to risks inherent in the market. But this is political scaremongering. U.S. citizens already utilize IRAs, 401(k)s, PCOs (portable cash options), Keoghs,

SEPs, and other investment options just fine, thank you. If some are conservative investors or managing for the short term, they direct their funds accordingly; if others are more inclined to take risks or are looking at the long run, they make appropriate decisions. Consumers already know how to invest their money—why does the government feel the need to patronize them when it comes to Social Security?

Let's stop here and revisit time inconsistency. Some may think that I am trying to have it both ways with consumers—that, on the one hand, I consider them so irrational that they have to be forced to save, yet, on the other hand, that they are rational enough to manage their own retirement accounts. But this view reveals a misunderstanding of the time-inconsistency problem. We need mandatory retirement accounts not because people are irrational, but precisely because they are *perfectly rational*—they know exactly what they are doing. If, for example, people know they will be cared for in old age—even if they don't save a nickel— then what is their incentive to save that nickel? Wouldn't it be rational to spend that nickel instead?

So, indeed, people are acting rationally when they choose not to save. We have rational people making choices based on the rules. The trick is to get the rules right. A mandatory retirement system, properly designed, would establish effective rules.

We would not be designing such a system out of whole cloth. About two dozen countries have reformed their state-run retirement programs, including Sweden, Australia, Peru, the United Kingdom, Kazakhstan, China, Croatia, and Poland. If citizens in these countries and many others can handle individual savings accounts, especially citizens in countries without a history of financial freedom, then U.S. citizens should be equally adept. At a time when the rest of the world is dropping the vestiges of state control, the United States should be leading the way and not lagging behind.

An important benefit of individual savings accounts is that they are transparent, and transparency solves many problems. For example, naysayers may point to the pension funds of such cities as San Diego and Minneapolis, which are currently struggling with underfunded pension plans. But these are pensions in which individuals have no control over their contributions and in which politicians, with the aid of accountants, can hide inadequate funding for a long period. The beauty of individual savings accounts is that each person decides how his money will be invested and can then monitor those investments at any time and easily make changes to react to changing investment news. (Those with Internet access can even do so on a daily basis.) Individual savings accounts are transparency in practice.

The benefits of such reform extend beyond the individual retirement accounts of U.S. citizens (although that would be reason enough for reform); they also accrue to the economy. As noted above, national savings will increase, as will participation in the labor force, both to the benefit of society. On the first point, more private assets means there will be more capital, which will have a positive impact on wages, which benefits the working people, especially the young. More capital also means the economy will have more productive assets, which also contributes to more production.

In terms of labor supply, any system that taxes people when they are young and gives it back when they are old will have a negative impact. People will simply work less. Put another way, if people are in control of their own savings, and if their retirement is funded by savings rather than transfers, they will work more because they will have more to gain. And everyone will be better off. Politicians and policymakers should be falling over themselves to accomplish these types of win-win situations.

And those policymakers need to get beyond the idea of creating only voluntary savings accounts. Voluntary accounts are not the full answer. There is nothing wrong with making a reasonable minimum level of savings mandatory. Remember that our current Social Security system is mandatory, but as it stands it is a mandatory tax that perpetuates a welfare system. It doesn't have to be this way. We should separate retirement savings from a system of welfare, and the most efficient way to do that is to turn our mandatory transfer system into a mandatory savings system. The part of the Social Security system that provides for disability and survivors insurance would not be rebuilt, just the part that provides for retirement.

Let's take a moment to discuss how such a system might look. First of all, consider the young worker under the current system. Early in life, when he is earning relatively lower wages, he is still forced to submit 5.3 percent of his wages to the care of older Americans, matched by his employer (which, of course, is really a tax on the worker's wages) for a total of 10.6 percent. At a time when that young worker could best put his resources toward human capital, like further education or a young family, or toward a mortgage or a car payment, he is forced to give up a significant portion of his relatively low wages. And again, he gets little in return for this tax, except a promise for some future return that may not even match current levels.

Now, consider a proposal that frees young workers from this tax and establishes rules to align older workers' incentives to solve the time-inconsistency problem, and it would look something like this:

- Before age twenty-five, workers would have no mandatory government retirement program.

- Beginning at age twenty-five, workers would contribute one-quarter of the retirement program (or roughly 3 percent, vis-à-vis the current 10.6 percent rate).

- At age thirty, that rate would increase to 5.3 percent.

- At thirty-five, the rate would equal the full 10.6 percent.

- At each step along the way, the worker would make choices about how a portion of his retirement account would be invested, much as that same worker would be making choices about his personal 401(k) or other investment options at work. (And, by the way, some companies are now forcing their employees to participate in retirement plans.)

- Upon retirement, this account would be used to provide payments over the remaining lives of the individual and spouse, if married.

This graduated move to full participation could also be achieved in a linear fashion with, say, a worker beginning at one-tenth participation in year one and then adding a tenth in subsequent years. The point here is not to present the perfect plan in all its detail, but to provide a means for rethinking our Social Security system. (Of course, some young workers will be better off than others and thus may choose to invest in other retirement programs on their own; this graduated government program would not preclude them from making other investment choices.)

Shouldn't we be worried, though, about people making bad choices with these retirement accounts and gambling all their savings on risky stocks, thereby making them wards of the state anyway? We should be no more worried about this happening than we are worried about federal workers gambling away their Thrift Plans. The reason we don't worry about federal workers playing roulette with their retirement accounts is that we don't let them—we have designed a system that allows individuals to make reasoned choices based on relatively conservative indexed options. The notion that people will be gambling away their retirement accounts on risky individual stocks is a red herring. People could make riskier choices with other investment resources; such "gambling" would simply not be an option under a rebuilt Social Security program.

The same holds true for that other red herring—that individual retirement accounts will simply line the pockets of Wall Street financial firms eager to charge exorbitant transaction fees to unsuspecting rubes. Again, we need look no further than the federal government's own Thrift Plan to see a low-fee retirement plan with conservative indexed options. Another benefit of these plans is that they allow people to manage their accounts online.

Some analysts have suggested that we cannot move from a transfer system to a savings system because current retirees will be left in the lurch. Who will pay for them if workers' money is suddenly shifted to individual savings accounts? There will indeed be a period of time, likely no more than ten years, when narrowly defined government debt relative to gross national income will increase before decreasing. But government debt is small relative to the present value of Social Security's expected promises in excess of expected future taxes summed over all individuals who currently exist. Further, the sum of the value of government debt and the value of these promises will start declining immediately.

Under a reformed system, there will always be some individuals who, owing to disabilities or other reasons that prevent them from working, will not have sufficient savings in their old age. The solution is to include a means-tested supplement to ensure that all citizens receive a required payment—just as they do today. Nobody gets left behind under this new system, and most will move ahead. U.S. citizens deserve more than a minimum payment, and the U.S. economy deserves more than to have its savings, capital, and labor weighed down by an increasingly costly tax-and-transfer system.

Reforming Social Security into a system of mandatory individual savings accounts is not as radical as it sounds. The world is moving in this direction, and U.S. citizens have been dealing with individual accounts for many years through their employers—and some of these accounts are mandatory.

Rebuild Social Security, Don't Reform It

No sooner did talk get serious about fixing Social Security than the political boo-birds went to work scaring people away from new ideas. It's rare to open a newspaper editorial page and not find someone screeching about evil policymakers and cranky politicians who are trying to destroy Social Security. Why a politician from any party would intentionally want to destroy a retirement program meant to benefit the elderly is beyond me. Such political claptrap makes me glad I'm an economist. Granted, politics is a game with its own rules and incentives, and people will rationally play by those rules for political gain, but such political role-playing certainly complicates matters, at best, and makes for bad policy, at worst.

Maybe one way to help avoid ad hominem attacks and political labeling would be to recast the Social Security question from one of reform to one of reconstruction. Let's not reform Social Security; let's rebuild it. In other words, if we could wipe the slate clean, what kind of retirement program would we build from scratch—today? It's one thing to snipe at new proposals, but it takes a plan to beat a plan, and I'm willing to bet that the best minds of both political parties, given such a charge, would not come up with a government retirement program as it currently exists.

We have had a lot of experience with our current Social Security system. We have had a lot of experience with other tax programs. And we have new insights into the effect of tax rates on labor supply. As that old maxim suggests, it's time we put that experience and insight to use and make good policy.

References

Bergoeing, Raphael, Patrick J. Kehoe, Timothy J. Kehoe, and Raimundo Soto. 2002. A Decade Lost and Found: Mexico and Chile in the 1980s. *Review of Economic Dynamics* 5 (1): 166–205.

Hayashi, Fumio, and Edward C. Prescott. 2002. The 1990s in Japan: A Lost Decade. *Review of Economic Dynamics* 5 (1): 206–35.

Prescott, Edward C. 2002. Prosperity and Depression. *American Economic Review* 92 (2): 1–15.

———. 2004. Why Do Americans Work So Much More than Europeans? *Federal Reserve Bank of Minneapolis Quarterly Review* 28 (1): 2–15.

Schettkat, Ronald. 2003. Differences in US-German Time-Allocation: Why Do Americans Work Longer Hours than Germans? *IZA Discussion Papers* 697. Institute for the Study of Labor (IZA).

9

My Beautiful Tax Reform

Joel Slemrod

Although he was most certainly not speaking of tax policy, Ralph Waldo Emerson might just as well have been when he wrote, in *The Conduct of Life*: "We ascribe beauty to that which is simple; which has no superfluous parts; which exactly answers its end" (Emerson 1860). The idea that simplicity is beautiful has often been embraced by artists and writers. Many scientists have argued that simplicity leads us to *truth*. Indeed, the Nobel laureate physicist Richard Feynman (1965) said one "can recognize truth by its beauty and simplicity." The Nobel physics prize winner four years after Feynman, Murray Gell-Mann (1964), said that in physics, "A chief criterion for the selection of a correct hypothesis . . . seems to be the criterion of beauty, simplicity, or elegance." Social scientists and certainly economists generally admire, and aspire to, the rigor of natural science. In tax policy, many experts equate the best tax system with the simplest, and the best tax reform with the one that most simplifies the system. But for many reasons, in economic and tax policy the simplest, most elegant policy need not be the best.

One reason is that tax policy involves a tradeoff among objectives, including equity and efficiency objectives, and often, achieving equity and efficiency requires some complexity. For example, at first blush the simplest tax system is what economists call a lump-sum tax, where the tax liability (not the tax rate) is the same for everyone, but not linking a family's tax liability to its level of well-being will certainly violate most people's, if not everyone's, concept of what is fair. This illustrates that determining the best tax policy depends not only on an understanding of economics, but also on values.

Because my favored tax system depends both on my economic assumptions and on my value judgments, which not everyone shares, saying exactly what tax reform I favor without laying out what leads me to this choice would not contribute much to the public policy debate. Thus, in what follows I will try to lay out explicitly what has led me to my viewpoint, so the reader can get a sense of how his own economics or values would lead to a different policy prescription.[1]

First, I believe we should seek the best (to be defined more carefully as I go along) tax system, not the worst. This may sound obvious, but it is not. Some people who believe that the government wastes most of the money it raises have argued that the tax system should purposely be made inefficient in order to limit how much tax revenue can be collected (Becker and Mulligan 2003). I disagree strongly with this point of view. If spending restraint is the objective, there are less costly ways to achieve it than by purposely running an inefficient tax system.

There are also serious practical obstacles to achieving an ideal system. Among other things, a tax system is a vast bureaucracy of collection and enforcement. This is important because no government can simply announce a tax system, sit back, and wait for the money to roll in. At first, most tax obligations would be remitted by citizens who are dutiful or not convinced that the IRS has really been dismantled. But after a while, the dutiful citizens would begin to feel like suckers, and the wary citizens would accept that there were no consequences from flouting the law. Revenue would dry up. Even a half-hearted attempt to enforce the tax system favors the amoral and aggressive.

Practical considerations are critical in assessing a tax reform that some argue is beautiful in its simplicity—replacing the federal income tax with a national retail sales tax (RST). This is, to be sure, a radical reform and also, at least at first glance, a radical simplification, in part because no individuals would have to file tax returns. Some supporters of the RST argue that adopting it would allow us to abolish the IRS.

If simple is beautiful, from afar the RST looks beautiful, indeed. But this is deceiving. First, keep in mind that the tax rate needed to replace federal income tax collections fully would be jaw-dropping, but not in a good way—about 27 percent if the federal sales tax base were the same as that of the average state, and considerably higher if the base did not include purchases of business inputs, as it should not. Add to that current state and local sales tax rates, maybe doubled to account for the fact that few states will maintain their income tax if the feds have abandoned theirs, and the rate would be well over 30 percent. Under a 30 percent–plus RST, the enforcement problems would be different than now, to be sure, but not smaller. All of the collection onus falls on one business sector for which the other side of the taxed transactions—consumers—has no incentive to help enforce the tax. Indeed, I believe it would be impossible to levy such a tax at the standards of equity and intrusiveness to which we are accustomed. Undoubtedly for these reasons, only six countries have operated an RST at a rate over 10 percent, and all but one has since abandoned it. I am a risk-averse person and would not bet the fiscal integrity of the United States on an untested—or more precisely, a tested-but-found-to-be-wanting—system of collecting revenue.

Unless, of course, I *wanted* to blow a (bigger) hole in the budget. But I do not. The tactic of "starving the beast" that is the federal government with big tax cuts has so far proven to be a failure. The resulting deficits lower national saving at a time when the country should be saving more to pre-pare for the retirement of the baby boom generation. This is an issue of intergenerational fairness, because it puts off assigning the tax burden to the future. We current taxpayers could soften the tax blow on our children by saving more and passing more along to them, but the evidence suggests that few people think this way (and many are too constrained to act even if they did think this way), and so by spending more than it takes in, the govern-ment is encouraging a spending spree at the expense of future generations. Tax reform should not be an occasion to worsen this problem.

Although a national retail sales tax looks beautiful only from afar, it has a more attractive sister called the value-added tax (VAT), which is now operated by more than one hundred countries. The VAT has a key administrative advantage over the RST in that it is collected from not only retail businesses but all businesses, and can have a clever self-enforcing feature that improves compliance. Some countries that levy a VAT raise nearly as much money, as a percentage of GDP, from it as the United States now raises from its income tax. It is not without its problems and com-plexities; the cost of compliance is not trivial, but is still probably half or less of that of our income tax.

In spite of the fact that a VAT promises considerable simplification over the current system, the VAT should not be a substitute for the income tax. I believe the government has an obligation to consider how its policies affect not only the dollar sum of GDP, but also whether the total is equitably shared. There is no value-neutral or self-evidently beautiful way to assign tax burdens. I favor a distribution of tax burdens in which the tax burden, as a proportion of income, should rise as income rises—what economists call *progressivity* of the tax burden. Not only should Bill Gates have a higher tax burden than a single mother earning $10,000 a year, but his tax burden as a fraction of his income should be higher (much higher, in my opinion). This conclusion reflects both my values and my economics. Where my values come from is not relevant, nor could I convince anyone to embrace my values. As for my economics, I recognize that a progressive tax distribution requires higher marginal tax rates, which dampen the incentive to work and do anything else that engenders financial success, and encourage privately rewarding but socially inefficient activities that reduce taxable income. But my reading of the empirical evidence has convinced me that the efficiency cost of progressivity is not so large (a professional judgment) that it overwhelms the benefits of a more equal distribution of well-being that tax progressivity provides (a value judgment).

Business-based tax systems such as the RST and the VAT cannot, on their own, deliver enough progressivity for me. Yes, both systems can exempt commodities, such as food, that comprise a higher percentage of the consumption basket of low-income families. But this is a very inefficient way to deliver progressivity, for the simple reason that not only low-income families buy food, and one that is incapable of delivering a program such as the earned income credit. One could couple an RST or a VAT with universal payments to families, but that would require an even higher rate of tax as well as a vast transfer-paying bureaucracy.

Enter the flat tax. By flat tax I do not mean any tax system that features one and only one tax rate. (If this were true, then both an RST and a VAT would qualify.) I mean *the* flat tax first proposed by Robert Hall and Alvin Rabushka (1983) in the early 1980s. This flat tax is really a VAT, with two related modifications. First, unlike a VAT, under the flat tax, businesses can deduct from the tax base payments to employees; second, employees are subject to tax on their labor income at the same rate of tax faced by businesses. These alterations do not imply much change at all in who remits tax to the government, because businesses could continue to withhold and remit the employees' tax liability. They do, though, require 100 million or so employees to file tax returns when they otherwise would not, which, to put it mildly, seems like an unnecessary administrative expense.

Why do it, then? Introducing the notion of individual tax liability facilitates introducing progressivity into the assignment of the tax burden. The Hall-Rabushka flat tax proposal takes advantage of this opportunity in one way only—it allows a standard deduction and personal exemptions, so there is an exempt level of labor income, which varies by family size. It then applies a single rate to all *labor* income above this level. In principle, though, there is no reason that a graduated tax rate schedule cannot be applied to the flat tax personal base. David Bradford has proposed exactly that, in what he calls the X tax, a name which has an air of mystery about it, to be sure, but arguably is less prone to confusion than calling it a "graduated flat tax" (Bradford 1996).

Having a separate personal tax allows something other than progressivity—the personalization of the tax burden. But having created the possibility, the creators of the flat tax do not partake. They allow no deductions, other than the standard deduction and personal exemptions— none. No deduction for mortgage interest, no deduction for charitable contributions, no child care credits, no tuition credits, and so on. But personalizing the tax system facilitates its use as a vehicle for an unlimited number of social and economic policies, incentives to particular behaviors, and rewards to particular constituencies. The prospect of eliminating *all* of these incentives and rewards is exhilarating to someone who seeks simplicity and beauty in a tax system, but is Pollyannaish to those who understand the American political system and the rewards showered on those politicians who control the dispensation of these goodies.

This is the issue that separates the tax-reform men from the tax-reform boys concerning the most fundamental of all questions—the extent of government involvement in the economy. Many conservatives who pay lip service to limited government get cold feet when it comes to sweeping away the interventions that occur via the tax system. I believe that, besides ensuring progressivity, the government's role in the economy should be limited. Not doing this inflicts costs in equity, efficiency, and complexity. Moreover, even in a time when more and more people use, or hire accountants who use, tax-preparation software, a complex tax system erodes the transparency of the fiscal relationship between government and citizens, at a cost to an informed participatory democracy.

Putting aside whether extensive government intervention is a good idea in principle, whether one should favor in practice cleaning up the current U.S. personal income tax base certainly depends on whether on balance one approves of the particular web of incentives and rewards that now exists. I am inclined to sweep the system pretty thoroughly, getting rid of many of the big items and most of the little items. In this chapter, I have the space to address only a few examples. Consider the itemized deduction for state and local income and property taxes, extended in the 2004 tax bill to state income or sales tax for the tax years 2004 and 2005. It is a subsidy for subfederal government expenditures at a rate that increases with the affluence of the jurisdictions' residents, because more affluent taxpayers are both more likely to itemize their deductions in the first place and, if they do, are likely to be subject to higher marginal tax rates, which is the effective rate of subsidy. It would never (and should not) be approved by Congress as a stand-alone subsidy program.

The same problem applies to the current preferential tax treatment of employer-provided health insurance, under which, unlike for cash compensation, health insurance expenditures are deductible to employers but not taxable to employees. This makes providing compensation in the form of health insurance significantly more attractive than it otherwise would be, and especially so for high-income taxpayers, and creates strong incentives for employers to offer more generous health benefits than otherwise. I favor capping or eliminating this tax preference, although this action should be taken only as part of a larger health-care reform effort that does not weaken the incentive for employers to provide group insurance plans without providing a viable health insurance alternative.

I favor abandoning the huge subsidy to owner-occupied housing implicit in the income tax but do not have an easy way to accomplish this (just eliminating the mortgage-interest deduction will not do the trick because the return to the housing asset remains untaxed, and self-financed owners are treated better than those who must take out a mortgage). Credit programs for education should be consolidated and simplified. The same goes for credits aimed at low-income families, which probably should be converted into a "standard credit" along the lines of the standard deduction, which eliminates the need for most families to itemize and document their eligibility for a host of programs with similar objectives. Those itemized deductions that remain should be turned into a credit at the first, basic income tax rate of about 15 percent.

If the tax base could be significantly cleaned up, it could achieve one of the key selling points of an RST—(most) individuals would not have to file tax returns. The British and Japanese income tax systems work this way now, and the U.S. Treasury Department has said it could work in the United States, too. It requires that the tax system be simplified enough that employer withholding can be exact for most taxpayers, meaning that little or no reconciliation by the individual is required. A no-individual-return, business-based system can be both progressive and personalized to the extent that employees (or third parties) provide employers with the information needed to calculate correctly how much tax to remit to the IRS on behalf of the employee. But ultimately, it must be the employee's responsibility to verify the accuracy of the information used to calculate tax liability, so that even though individuals might not file returns, they will in some way have to be involved in the tax collection system. A highly personalized no-individual-return system requires that individuals provide their employers with information that currently goes to the government, which changes the locus but not the extent of intrusiveness.

Because of the withholding taxes that they remit on behalf of their employees, businesses are central to the process of taxing labor income. But, not surprisingly, businesses are also central to the taxation of business income, and they could be central to how we tax the income received by those who supply capital to businesses. How this works in the current system is a mess.

To see why, first consider how a progressive, comprehensive (i.e., all sources of income are subject to tax) income tax system should work. Business income would be attributed to the owners of the business and taxed at whatever rate is appropriate, given the total income of the owner. If nonowners have supplied capital to the business, the cost of obtaining the capital should be deducted from business income, and the income paid should be subject to tax at the appropriate tax rate of the supplier of the capital.

This is how it works now for all but the biggest public corporations. Any business with one hundred or fewer owners, which accounts for the vast majority of businesses, can retain the legal advantages of incorporation—principally limited liability and perpetual ownership—while paying no corporation income tax. The company's income is allocated to the owners and added to their individual taxable income. However, an incorporated business or, since 1997, even an unincorporated business can elect to be subject to the corporation income tax and its graduated rate structure, which subjects annual taxable income up to $75,000 to first a 15 percent and then a 25 percent rate. Although the graduated rate structure of the corporation income tax mimics the graduation of the personal tax, it cannot be justified on progressivity grounds, because the total income of the owner of the business may put him well into the top (currently 35 percent) individual bracket, so that the tax relief afforded by the lower corporate rates is unjustified. Thus, for the vast majority of businesses, the corporation tax is by no means a burdensome double tax; rather, it is an option for tax reduction. One of two changes should be made to this system: Restrict the ability of companies to be subject to the corporation rate structure, or eliminate the low rates of tax on the first $75,000 of income.

An entirely different system applies to the big, publicly owned companies that comprise only a few thousand of the several million businesses in the country but account for a large fraction of business activity. Publicly owned corporations cannot elect out of the corporation income tax. This produces an odd system in many ways. First, it subjects the corporation's income to what is effectively a flat rate of 35 percent (the tax benefits of the lower rates in the bottom brackets are trivial compared to the vast income of public corporations), regardless of what tax bracket the owners of the corporation are in, and regardless even of whether the shareholders are tax-exempt entities. Taxing big corporations by attributing business income directly to the shareholders would in principle solve these problems, but it raises formidable and probably insurmountable practical problems. Many other countries allow shareholders a partial credit for the taxes that corporations have already paid, approximating the way that employers withhold personal income tax for their employees, but with no attempt to adjust the amount of tax withheld and remitted by the business to the personal tax circumstances of the shareholders.

A second issue is that although the tax treatment of business borrowing is consistent with the ideal—interest payments are deductible as a business expense but taxable to the lender—the taxation of equity finance does not follow this pattern. The corporation is not allowed to deduct anything in recognition of the cost of attracting the financing, but the equity providers (i.e., the shareholders) are taxed to some degree on the income they receive. This system causes inefficient incentives for corporations to raise capital by borrowing and to manage payments from the corporation to the shareholders in tax-efficient, but otherwise inefficient, ways. Finally, the two levels of tax, corporate and individual, could cause the tax rate on business income to be higher than it is on other income and the cost of capital for corporate businesses to be higher than it is for other businesses, neither of which is justifiable.

The most sensible approach to these problems is to allow a personal tax credit to shareholders for some or all of corporation taxes paid. In 2003, the United States adopted a different approach when the personal tax rate on dividends and capital gains was capped at 15 percent, compared to a maximum 35 percent rate on other income. There are two problems with this approach. First, it moves the system toward one where the rate of tax on corporate income is 35 percent regardless of the tax situation of the owner, which is inconsistent with progressivity and certainly inconsistent with the oft-heralded idea of making stock ownership attractive to lower-income people. Second, it cuts the personal tax on corporate-source income while doing nothing to ensure that the corporate-level tax was in fact paid. Notably, the original Bush administration proposal in the 2003 legislation linked the two levels of tax by making dividends tax-free (and not just capped at 15 percent) only to the extent that the dividend-paying corporation had actually paid corporation tax. Linking the two taxes ensures that, in the quest for attaining a single level of tax on corporate income, we do not end up collecting no tax at all; this is an important policy issue in light of the apparent but difficult-to-document increase in abusive corporate tax shelter schemes that have drained corporation tax collections. This link, abandoned in the legislation that was eventually passed, should be revived by allowing a credit only for corporation taxes actually paid.

Apparently many public corporations opposed the link in the original 2003 proposal because it would reveal publicly that they paid little or no corporation income taxes. One might think that their financial statements would reveal this fact, but they do nothing of the kind, due to the myriad differences between accounting for book income and taxable income. To promote transparency of public policy, I believe public corporations should have to reveal how much tax they pay—not all the details of their tax return, which might reveal information helpful to competitors and reduce the informativeness of the tax return, but just the bottom line. In addition, the IRS should be allocated the resources it needs to investigate, and the courts should crack down on, abusive corporate tax shelters and avoidance schemes.

Finally, just as the personal tax base should be cleaned, so should the tax base be cleaned of tax loopholes carved out solely for specific companies or industries. These provisions generally have no principled economic justification—rather the beneficiaries are often the most politically connected—and therefore cause resources to flow to less efficient uses. A principled commitment to a less activist government requires leveling the playing field among businesses and, with only limited exceptions, letting private entrepreneurs and capital owners determine how the economy's resources are directed.

In sum, with my beautiful tax reform, business and capital income would be more systematically subject to progressive taxation, by eliminating the benefit of graduated corporation income tax rates, offering a credit for corporation taxes paid by tax-paying public corporations, and cleaning the corporate tax base. There are, to be sure, other intriguing proposals for rationalizing the taxation of business and capital income. For example, under the comprehensive business income tax (CBIT), both corporate dividends and interest payments are tax-free at the individual level but, in parallel, corporate interest payments are no longer a deductible business expense, putting them on a level playing field with dividends and eliminating the distortions to financial behavior the tax system now produces. Under the CBIT, all business income is taxed at 35 percent, as opposed to the current system, under which, for the vast majority of businesses, the income is taxed at the appropriate tax rate of the owner. As with the RST, the VAT, and the Hall-Rabushka flat tax, under a CBIT there is no distinction between corporations and other businesses.

The CBIT eliminates the tax consequences of payments of dividends and interest (to the payer and the recipient) made by businesses, but leaves them in place for other transactions, including mortgage interest payments. One could go farther and eliminate the tax consequences of all financial flows, as occurs under an RST, a VAT, or a Hall-Rabushka flat tax. This would not cost as much revenue as one might first guess because it would not only be exempt from tax receipts of interest, but it would also disallow interest deductions. Because the latter on net are taken by taxpayers in higher tax brackets than those who receive interest payments, attempting to collect revenue on financial flows raises little or no revenue in aggregate. Eliminating the tax consequences would eliminate a highly complex area of the tax law that tries to measure the taxable flow of a vast array of complicated financial instruments, such as zero-coupon bonds and swaps. Although I admit to being intrigued by this type of proposal, I do not support this type of reform because it raises serious unresolved issues regarding the transition from the current system and how well it would integrate with the tax systems of the rest of the world.

Note that I have now come full circle in my discussion of tax reform options. Requiring all businesses to pay tax at a single rate on a base with no deductions for interest payments and taking dividend and interest receipts out of a completely cleaned-up personal tax base is, with one important exception, exactly the Hall-Rabushka flat tax (or, with a graduated personal tax structure, the X tax). The one exception is that under an income tax or a CBIT, businesses must depreciate the purchase of capital goods, while under the flat tax they can immediately write off expenses. In this way, income of all types can be taxed at the business source of income. As noted, taxing (only) at the business source affords considerable simplicity but does not easily accommodate a progressive distribution of the tax burden.

Conclusion

Under my beautiful tax reform, most Americans would not have to file tax returns. The tax system would no longer be the primary source of goodies passed out by the government and a major determinant of how resources are allocated—what goodies and subsidies that remain would be consolidated. Progressivity would be retained with a system under which most, but not all, American taxpayers would be subject to a low, basic rate, the same rate at which all tax credits can be redeemed. Taxation of business income would be rationalized with the objective of taxing all business income at the appropriate tax rate of the income earner, sharply reducing tax sheltering, and making corporation tax payments more transparent.

I recognize that this system is not as beautiful as others that have been proposed, and that therefore the title of my chapter involves some irony. My tax reform is not more beautiful because beauty as simplicity is not the only criterion for choosing a tax system, and, alas, there are tradeoffs among the characteristics that matter to me. My desire for progressivity rules out entirely business-based systems. My desire to avoid serious unintended consequences means that tax systems that eliminate the tax consequences of financial flows will have to wait until the transitional and international implications are more fully worked out. By the standards of the scientist and philosopher Buckminster Fuller, who said that "when I have finished [working on a problem], if the solution is not beautiful, I know it is wrong," I have probably failed. But I take comfort in the words of perhaps the greatest of all scientists, Albert Einstein (1977), who once cautioned that "everything should be made as simple as possible, but not simpler."

Note

1. My views on tax policy are laid out in much more detail in Slemrod and Bakija (2004).

References

Becker, Gary S., and Casey B. Mulligan. 2003. Deadweight Costs and the Size of Government. *Journal of Law and Economics* 46 (October): 293–340.

Bradford, David F. 1996. *Fundamental Issues in Consumption Taxation*. Washington, D.C.: AEI Press.

Einstein, Albert. 1977. *Reader's Digest*. October.

Emerson, Ralph Waldo. 1860. *The Conduct of Life*. London: Smith, Elder, and Co.

Feynman, Richard. 1965. *The Character of Physical Law*. Cambridge, Mass.: MIT Press.

Fuller, Buckminster. Quotation available at http://www.geocities.com/baskarc/CBScientistsQuotes.htm.

Gell-Mann, Murray. 1964. Particles and Principles. *Physics Today* 17, no. 11 (November): 22.

Hall, Robert, and Alvin Rabushka. 1983. *Low Tax, Simple Tax, Flat Tax*. New York: McGraw-Hill.

Slemrod, Joel, and Jon Bakija. 2004. *Taxing Ourselves: A Citizen's Guide to the Debate over Taxes*. 3rd edition. Cambridge, Mass.: MIT Press.

Conclusion

Alan J. Auerbach and Kevin A. Hassett

We have seen in the preceding chapters that serious scholars have reached strikingly different conclusions concerning the most desirable structure of possible tax reforms. In this final chapter, we illuminate the key issues that divide opinion, drawing in part on conversations that occurred during an informal conference among these authors.

Inevitably, debate focuses on the gap between what is known and what would have to be known in order for the case for fundamental reform to be logically indisputable. If a large country like the United States (or even many such countries) had once had a tax system exactly like our own and then shifted to a flat consumption tax, one could base policy recommendations on precisely applicable experience.

Without such clear evidence, one must rely on models that link together many different small experiences and attempt to construct an informative whole. Confidence in this approach varies among economists. Since models are inevitably simplifications of reality, applying their predictions to the real world requires prudence. At what point is confidence in the economic method sufficient to merit firm policy prescriptions? As these chapters illustrate, the answer varies considerably, even among economists. So, as we begin to consider tax reform, what might a list of our assets and liabilities look like?

What Is "Known" and What Is Suspected?

As discussed in our introduction, a large theoretical literature documents a wide range of positive effects of a move toward either an income tax with a broader base and lower rates, or a consumption tax. Based on results from a fairly large number of different models, the literature suggests that a wholesale switch to an ideal system might eventually increase economic output by between 5 and 10 percent, or perhaps a slightly wider range.

There is little question that the typical informed reader would predict significantly improved economic performance from a rational tax reform. For example, in a survey of sixty-nine specialists in public finance published in 1998, Victor Fuchs and colleagues found that the median respondent believed GDP growth would have been one percentage point per year lower for a lengthy period after 1986 if the previously existing tax code had not been repealed. Since the code has evolved dramatically away from the relatively simple structure of 1986, one would guess that a similar potential for higher growth through reform exists today. Indeed, the survey's median projected long-run effect on output is well within the range of estimates of the theoretical models.

However, this consensus may exist because all the models employed by economists have relied upon some simplifying assumption that will eventually be found inappropriate. That is, it might well be that the models will be poor predictors of experience. Currently, a number of central European nations, as well as Hong Kong and the Channel Islands, are engaged in experiments with flat consumption taxes. Estonia, for example, has now relied upon one for a decade. Research is under way to identify the effects of these reforms after controlling for the unique characteristics of the countries that have adopted them, but until that literature is mature, policymakers will have to rely largely on theory.

To date, the best support for the models comes from more microeconomic evidence. For example, one of the potential benefits of a consumption tax is that it reduces the costs of making new investments in plants and equipment. If significant growth effects are to follow consumption-tax reform, they will depend in part on the investment response; and since taxes that affect investment have changed over time, experience with such "mini" tax reforms should be a useful guide in evaluating a larger reform. The evidence of these mini-reforms has been quite promising, and consistent with the movements one would project from the full-fledged tax-reform simulations. For example, a large literature generally has found that corporate investment decisions are highly responsive to taxes. (See Hassett and Hubbard 2002 for a recent review.)

But a number of complete and relevant experiments are needed to dispel uncertainty about the impact of reform—uncertainty especially troubling to those concerned with equity issues, since the direct impact of many of the reforms would be to raise the direct tax payments of those in the middle- and perhaps lower-income deciles. Tax reform might well have undesirable distributional implications, particularly if growth effects are disappointing. A widening of the after-tax distribution of resources that might be acceptable if all groups gained would be more troubling if there were little growth and, hence, losses among the less fortunate. On balance, then, a rational policymaker might respond to the model uncertainty by relying on a more progressive consumption tax than he might otherwise choose.

What Is Feasible?

Both broad-based income taxes and broad-based consumption taxes would improve the overall efficiency of the economy because the current code does so much to undermine it. For example, an efficient tax code affects the decisions of individuals as little as possible; yet the mortgage-interest deduction provides a very large subsidy to home ownership, and thus introduces a large economic distortion. If the political system is fully wedded to a virtually unlimited mortgage-interest deduction, many of the benefits of tax reform are unattainable. There are numerous other similar provisions in the code that are politically popular but have questionable economic merit.

Even if economists become convinced that full and immediate adoption of a progressive consumption tax would make everyone better off, such a reform may be politically impossible, and hence uninteresting. This view certainly is entertained by some of the participants in this volume. But economists should first decide whether they truly have reached a consensus on tax reform. Such a consensus would have some impact on the thinking of policymakers, many of whom employ and rely upon their advice.

Moreover, as more countries experiment with tax systems that are designed with an eye on the economic literature, the value of economics will be revealed eventually, one way or another. If, for instance, countries that adopt consumption taxes significantly outperform those that continue to rely on ornate and politically expedient substitutes, pressure for change will increase. This pressure will not intensify because the *American Economic Review* replaces *People* magazine on American coffee tables, but rather because superior economic performance has a demonstration effect. Thus, a reform in the near term will be more possible if economists continue to focus on reaching a consensus of what might be optimal without political constraints. In the long run, if economists are correct, economic forces may well move politicians away from their perceived constraints in any case, and reward those who overcome their constraints earlier.

Will the Benefits of Reform Be Long Lasting?
Can Steps Be Taken to Help Ensure They Are?

Related to the issue just raised, some have argued that even if the task of enacting reform is accomplished, it will be Sisyphean if politicians immediately begin undoing their own handiwork. This view was perhaps best expressed by Nobel laureate Milton Friedman, who argued that politicians might enact tax reforms simply to maximize their own happiness:

> The political function of the income taxes, which is served by their being complex, is to provide a means whereby the members of Congress who have anything whatsoever to do with taxation can raise campaign funds. That is what supports the army of lobbyists in Washington who are seeking to produce changes in the income tax, to introduce special privileges or exemptions for their clients, or to have what they regard as special burdens on their clients removed. A strict flat-rate tax would offer nothing that any lobbyist could hope to achieve since the structure of the tax is so simple and straightforward (Friedman 1995).

In such a world, politicians peddle special tax favors to various interest groups and campaign contributors. After many years of such activity, the tax code becomes so complex that it is difficult to add new favors. At that point, the slate may be wiped clean again, but only so the process begins anew.

Given the sad evolution of the tax code since 1986, this concern is very serious. One could add to it a second concern raised by Casey Mulligan in this volume. In 2003, he and Gary Becker found that more efficient taxes (like VATs) have tended to increase more often over time than less efficient taxes. Thus, tax reform might have two possible political paths. If a simplified, broad-based income tax is adopted—as it was in 1986—it will gradually become more complex, eventually undoing all of the benefits of reform. If a simplified consumption tax is adopted (like a VAT), it may be difficult to add ornate tax candy to the code, but increasing the tax rate itself will be easier, and politicians may engage in more spending, not all of which is necessarily desirable.

If these two paths encompassed the entire range of possibilities, then it would be difficult to get excited about tax reform. Indeed, to the extent that repeated changes in the tax code introduce uncertainty, it might even be better to stop the process Friedman envisages of repeated tax reforms and just resign oneself to accepting the code we have, and at least eliminate the uncertainty. This appears to be a temptation for some of the authors in this volume.

Accordingly, it is important that any attempt at fundamental tax reform address these issues head-on. If efficient taxes encourage wasteful spending, are there better alternatives to keeping a distortionary tax system? Evidence from the states suggests the answer may be yes. A careful study of their history, for example, has revealed that supermajority requirements have significantly reduced taxes in the states that have adopted them (Knight 2000). One could imagine, then, a reform accompanied by a rule that any modification of the tax base or tax rate require a supermajority vote in both houses. For this rule to be truly binding, however, it would have to be a constitutional amendment, the conditions necessary to accomplish which are quite strenuous.

In the absence of such a large change, it is worth noting that budget rules limiting spending have been found in an extensive literature, again for U.S. states, to have been effective (Poterba 1997). Since some were passed with simple majorities, it is possible to conceive of constraints that could be effective at the federal level without a constitutional amendment. The experience under different federal budget rules, beginning with the Gramm-Rudman-Hollings legislation of the 1980s and the discretionary spending caps and "PAYGO" rules of the 1990s, suggests that such budget rules have some impact, but also that designing effective ones is quite difficult. It is challenging to place hard limits on spending, and it is equally challenging to find the right balance between curtailing wasteful spending and allowing spending that may be socially beneficial.

More on the Risks of Relying on Economic Models

Two additional considerations must be made as one weighs the relative evidence on the impact of tax reform. First, the literature that has found the impact of tax reform to be in the range we mentioned has generally assumed that marginal tax rates have a moderate impact on the labor effort of workers. This assumption has been based on a voluminous literature that has used detailed data on the behavior of individual workers to identify the impact of tax policy on effort. This assumption moderates the estimated economic benefits of tax reform, because the high marginal rates of the current code have only a measured negative impact on work effort.

However, the recent work by Edward C. Prescott discussed by him in his chapter has suggested that labor supply may respond to changes in the tax code far more in the long run than previously believed. These long-run responses appear present in the macroeconomic data, and may occur over a longer horizon than could have been studied with the individual-level data upon which the previous literature relied.

An example of the evidence that Prescott's work has identified is that European workers generally worked as many hours as Americans in the 1960s, when our tax rates were relatively similar. Since then, rates in the United States have declined and rates in Europe have gone up, and hours worked have diverged dramatically. A recent paper independently supports these results and relates them to taxes more specifically (Davis and

Henrekson 2004). In particular, the authors argue that high taxes on labor encourage individuals to substitute home production for tasks that might be farmed out in low-tax nations. Since high taxes make it more expensive to hire workers, individuals in high-tax countries might be more likely to paint their own kitchens and mow their own lawns. Their workweek will look shorter, because it measures work for an employer, but it will not really be shorter. More of it will be allocated to unmeasured home activities. The authors found strong evidence of exactly this type of pattern in the data. German workers, for example, have shorter work-weeks, but rely far less on contractors to perform household duties.

Accordingly, one must entertain some possibility that the estimates in the literature to date are on the low side because they are based on an underestimate of the possible labor-supply response to lower taxes. To help shed light on the possible impact of this change, we incorporated a labor response similar to that supported by Prescott into a standard Auerbach-Kotlikoff model that has been very often used in the literature. We found that the higher elasticity increased the estimated effect of tax reform by more than a factor of two, with long-run output increasing after a switch to a consumption tax by 25 percent. As one balances the risks of relying on the current literature, this is an important consideration.

On the other hand, another issue that arose in discussion at the conference suggests additional risks in applying the literature to the real world, pointing in the other direction. In particular, the chapter by R. Glenn Hubbard argues that the distributional impact of a consumption tax is much smaller than has been believed because the difference between a consumption tax and an income tax is smaller than has been believed. Hubbard argues that both tax excessive returns on capital, but that the consumption tax excludes from taxation the opportunity cost of capital, which is much lower.

As a technical matter this is true. If Microsoft, for example, purchases a CD-stamping machine to increase its output of Windows software, then the profit it obtains from that output will certainly include excess profits associated with the unique market position of that company. Mechanically, in a consumption tax, Microsoft reduces its tax by deducting the cost of the CD-stamping machine, but that is tiny compared to its profits. The difference is taxed.

Here is where a problem applying the existing literature is raised, however. The existing literature has assumed that one removes the tax on *all* of the return on capital when one moves from an income tax to a consumption tax. Thus, the change that has been studied may be significantly larger than the change that actually would occur during a fundamental reform. If so, then the estimates of the economic benefits may be too high.

A full understanding of this issue requires additional modeling efforts that have been done only sparingly in the literature to date. There are many possible reasons a firm might earn high profits—patents, monopoly, and even corruption come to mind—and a full-fledged model of these forces would be required to understand the full impact of tax reform. However, as observed in a celebrated article by Joan Robinson in 1933, a firm that raises its price because of patent or other monopoly power is effectively imposing a tax. Thus, taxes by the federal government may be far more distortionary in a world where firms charge higher prices and earn higher noncompetitive profits. This point was driven home quite forcefully by Kenneth Judd (2000), who showed that capital taxes may be far more economically damaging in a world where firms charge prices well above their cost.

Thus, on the one hand, the Hubbard observation might suggest that the literature has overestimated the true effective change if there is a consumption-tax reform. On the other hand, these models have ignored a factor pushing in the other direction by excluding from their analysis the economic distortions associated with high profits.

There is a long list of other factors that have mostly been excluded from models to date. On balance, a reading of this literature suggests to us that the range of economic effects we have described for the core literature is reasonable to consider when contemplating the likely benefits of reform.

What Would Tax Reform Deliver?

The chapters in this book provide a detailed glimpse of the current state of the art in the study of tax reform. Economic models suggest that the benefits of fundamental reform may be large. However, reform is a somewhat delicate thing. If politically popular provisions such as the mortgage-interest deduction remain after the reform, then the benefits will have been largely squandered. If reformers do not build safeguards that prohibit future tinkering with their reform, they may find that much of their effort is of only temporary benefit.

As conversations among the scholars assembled at our conference probed toward decisive differences, the most telling ones clearly involved value judgments concerning the merits of redistribution, and professional judgments concerning the likelihood that the efforts of economic scribblers accurately portray the impact of a reform enacted in the real world. In particular, unease that the economic effects may be smaller than advertised interacted with unease concerning a flattening of direct redistribution.

Accordingly, one could say that if anything close to a consensus could be reached among economists it might be that a tax reform should involve an expanded role for consumption taxation and should err in the direction of being at least distributionally neutral as measured directly. Rather than rely on a flat tax, one might take the more progressive version of it proposed by David F. Bradford in chapter 1. In his tax, rates on consumption start at zero for the lowest income brackets and climb to about 30 percent for those in the highest brackets. Given that the tax has a number of possible rates, reasonable individuals ought to be able to use it as a basic structure within which uncertainty about the economic benefits of reform is hedged by lowering rates on those at the bottom and raising them on those at the top. Again, simulations have suggested that a good bit of the benefit of a flat tax is obtainable with such a reform.

That voluminous research should move the profession toward a consensus concerning an approach first proposed by Bradford decades ago is a fitting testament to the lasting contribution of the man to whom this book is dedicated, and a fitting conclusion to this book.

References

Altig, David, Alan J. Auerbach, Laurence J. Kotlikoff, Kent A. Smetters, and Jan Walliser. 2001. Simulating Fundamental Tax Reform in the United States. *American Economic Review* 91 (3): 574–95.

Becker, Gary S., and Casey B. Mulligan. 2003. Deadweight Costs and the Size of Government. *Journal of Law and Economics* 46 (2): 293–340.

Davis, Steven J., and Magnus Henrekson. 2004. Tax Effects on Work Activity, Industry Mix and Shadow Economy Size: Evidence from Rich-Country Comparisons. NBER Working Paper 10509, May. www.nber.org/papers/w10509 (accessed April 7, 2005).

Friedman, Milton. 1995. Why a Flat Tax Is Not Politically Feasible. *Wall Street Journal*. March 30.

Fuchs, Victor R., Alan B. Krueger, and James M. Poterba. 1998. Economists' Views about Parameters, Values, and Policy: Survey Results in Labor and Public Finance. *Journal of Economic Literature* 36 (3): 1387–1425.

Hassett, Kevin A., and R. Glenn Hubbard. 2002. Tax Policy and Investment. In Alan Auerbach and Martin Feldstein, eds. *Handbook of Public Economics*. Vol. 3. Amsterdam, The Netherlands: North-Holland.

Judd, Kenneth L. 2000. The Impact of Tax Reform in Modern Dynamic Economies. In Kevin Hassett and R. Glenn Hubbard, eds. *Transition Costs of Fundamental Tax Reform*. Washington D.C.: AEI Press.

Knight, Brian G. 2000. Supermajority Voting Requirements for Tax Increases: Evidence from the States. *Journal of Public Economics* 76 (1): 41–67.

Poterba, James, M. 1997. Do Budget Rules Work? In Alan J. Auerbach, ed. *Fiscal Policy: Lessons from Economic Research*. Cambridge, Mass.: MIT Press.

Robinson, Joan. 1933. *The Economics of Imperfect Competition*. London: Macmillan and Company.

Index

About the Authors

Alan J. Auerbach is Robert D. Burch Professor of Economics and Law, director of the Burch Center for Tax Policy and Public Finance, and former chairman of the Economics Department at the University of California–Berkeley. He is also a research associate of the National Bureau of Economic Research in Cambridge, Massachusetts. Previously, he taught at Harvard University and the University of Pennsylvania and was deputy chief of staff of the Joint Committee on Taxation of the U.S. Congress. Professor Auerbach has been a consultant to several government agencies and institutions in the United States and abroad. He has served as a member of the Executive Committee and as vice president of the American Economic Association, and is a fellow of the Econometric Society and of the American Academy of Arts and Sciences.

David F. Bradford was professor of economics and public affairs at Princeton University, adjunct professor of law at New York University, and adjunct scholar at the American Enterprise Institute. He was a research associate at the National Bureau of Economic Research in Cambridge, Massachusetts, where for a number of years he directed the program of research in taxation, and he was also a research fellow in the CESifo (Germany) research network. Dr. Bradford previously was deputy assistant secretary for tax policy in the U.S. Department of the Treasury, where he directed a study resulting in the published volume, *Blueprints for Basic Tax Reform*, which is widely regarded as the forerunner of the major income-tax reform enacted in 1986. From 1991 to 1993, Dr. Bradford served as a member of the President's Council of Economic Advisers, working in such policy areas as the environment, telecommunications, health care, and financial institutions and taxation. Dr. Bradford's research for most of his career, including his 1986 book, *Untangling the Income Tax*, centered on public-sector economics, especially taxation. As illustrated by the present work, he maintained his lifelong interest in taxation, but in recent years, environmental teaching and research were his principal preoccupations. Dr. Bradford passed away on February 22, 2005.

William G. Gale is a senior fellow and holds the Arjay and Frances Miller Chair in Federal Economic Policy in the Economic Studies Program at the Brookings Institution. He is deputy director of the Economic Studies Program and codirector of the Tax Policy Center, a joint venture of the Brookings Institution and the Urban Institute. His areas of expertise include tax policy, budget and fiscal policy, and public and private saving behavior and pensions. Before joining Brookings, Mr. Gale was an assistant professor in the Department of Economics at the University of California–Los Angeles and served as a senior staff economist for the Council of Economic Advisers. He has also served as a consultant to the General Accounting Office and the World Bank. He is the coeditor of *Private Pensions and Public Policy* (2004); *Rethinking Estate and Gift Taxation* (2001); *Economic Effects of Fundamental Tax Reform* (1996); and *The Evolving Pension System: Trends, Effects, and Proposals for Reform* (forthcoming), all published by Brookings.

Michael J. Graetz is the Justus S. Hotchkiss Professor of Law at Yale University. Before becoming a professor at Yale in 1983, he was a professor of law at the University of Virginia and the University of Southern California law schools, and a professor of law and social sciences at the California Institute of Technology. Mr. Graetz has served as assistant to the secretary and special counsel at the Department of the Treasury, as Treasury deputy assistant secretary for tax policy, and on the Internal Revenue Service commissioner's Advisory Group. Additionally, Mr. Graetz has been a John Simon Guggenheim Memorial Fellow and has received an award from *Esquire* magazine for courses and work in connection with providing shelter for the homeless. His publications on the subject of federal taxation include a leading law school text and more than fifty articles on a wide range of tax, health policy, social insurance, and tax compliance issues. His most recent books include *True Security: Rethinking Social*

Insurance (Yale University Press, 1999) and *The U.S. Income Tax: What It Is, How It Got That Way and Where We Go from Here* (W. W. Norton & Company, 1999). Articles Mr. Graetz has authored include "The 'Original Intent' of U.S. International Taxation" (*Duke Law Journal*, 1997) and "Taxing International Income: Inadequate Principles, Outdated Concepts and Unsatisfactory Policies" (*Tax Law Review*, 2001).

Robert E. Hall is the Robert and Carole McNeil Professor of Economics and senior fellow at Stanford University. Mr. Hall is an applied economist with interests in technology, competition, employment issues, and economic policy in the aggregate economy and in particular markets. His current research focuses on levels of activity and employment and stock-market valuations in market economies and on the economics of high technology. Mr. Hall is a member of the National Academy of Sciences, a fellow of the American Academy of Arts and Sciences, and a fellow of the Econometric Society. Before coming to Stanford University in 1978, Mr. Hall taught at the Massachusetts Institute of Technology and at the University of California–Berkeley. He has advised a number of government agencies on national economic policy, including the Justice Department, the Department of the Treasury, and the Federal Reserve Board, and served on the National Presidential Advisory Committee on Productivity. Mr. Hall currently serves as director of the National Bureau of Economic Research's research program on economic fluctuations and growth, an interuniversity research organization, and is chairman of the bureau's Committee on Business Cycle Dating. Mr. Hall has worked with Hoover Institution colleague Alvin Rabushka to develop a comprehensive tax reform based on a flat tax, which the two wrote about first in December 1981 in an influential article in the *Wall Street Journal*, and more extensively in their book, *The Flat Tax* (Hoover Institution Press, 1995). Mr. Hall is coauthor, with Marc Lieberman, of *Economics: Principles and Applications* (South Western, 1997).

Kevin A. Hassett is director of economic policy studies and resident scholar at the American Enterprise Institute. Before joining AEI, Mr. Hassett was a senior economist at the Board of Governors of the Federal Reserve System and an associate professor of economics and finance at the Graduate School of Business at Columbia University. He was an economic advisor to the Bush campaign in the 2004 presidential election, and was the chief economic advisor to Senator John McCain (R-Ariz.) during the 2000 primaries. He also served as a policy consultant to the U.S. Department of the Treasury during both the former Bush and Clinton administrations. Mr. Hassett is a member of the Joint Committee on Taxation's Dynamic Scoring Advisory Panel. He is the author, coauthor, or editor of six books on economics and economic policy. He has published scholarly articles in the *American Economic Review*, the *Economic Journal*, the *Quarterly Journal of Economics*, the *Review of Economics and Statistics*, the *Journal of Public Economics*, and many other professional journals. His popular writings have been published in the *Wall Street Journal*, the *Atlantic Monthly*, *USA Today*, the *Washington Post*, and numerous other outlets. His economic commentaries are regularly aired on radio and television, including recent appearances on the *Today Show*, the CBS *Morning Show*, the *NewsHour with Jim Lehrer*, *Hardball*, *Moneyline*, and *Power Lunch*.

R. Glenn Hubbard is dean of the Graduate School of Business at Columbia University and a visiting scholar at AEI. His research spans tax policy, monetary economics, corporate finance, and international finance. Mr. Hubbard has been a member of the Columbia University faculty since 1988 and is currently the Russell L. Carson Professor of Finance and Economics. He served as the codirector of the Entrepreneurship Program at Columbia from 1998 to 2004. He has been a visiting professor at the John F. Kennedy School of Government, Harvard Business School, and the University of Chicago. Professor Hubbard also held the John M. Olin Fellowship at the National Bureau of Economic Research and remains affiliated with the bureau's research programs on monetary economics, public economics, corporate finance, and industrial organization. Mr. Hubbard served as deputy assistant secretary for tax policy at the U.S. Department of the Treasury from 1991 to 1993. He supervised administration efforts on revenue estimates, tax reform, and health policy. From 2001 to 2003, he was chairman of the U.S. Council of Economic Advisers under President George W. Bush. His responsibilities included advising the president on economic policy, tax and budget policy, emerging market financial issues, international finance, health care, and environmental policy. While serving as CEA chairman, he also chaired the Economic Policy Committee of the OECD.

Casey B. Mulligan is a professor in the Department of Economics at the University of Chicago. He has also served as a visiting professor of public economics at Harvard University, Clemson University, and the Irving B. Harris Graduate School of Public Policy Studies at the University of Chicago. He is affiliated with a number of professional organizations, including the National Bureau of Economic Research, the George J. Stigler Center for the Study of the Economy and the State, and the Population Research Center. He is also the recipient of numerous awards and fellowships, including those from the National Science Foundation, the Alfred P. Sloan Foundation, the Smith-Richardson Foundation, and the John M. Olin Foundation. He is author of *Parental Priorities and Economic Inequality* (University of Chicago Press, 1997), which studies economic models of, and statistical evidence on, the intergenerational transmission of economic status. His recent research is concerned with capital and labor taxation, with particular emphasis on tax incidence and positive theories of public policy. His recent work in progress includes *Social Security in Theory and Practice* (a book with Columbia Professor Xavier Sala-i-Martin). Mr. Mulligan has been published in the *Chicago Tribune*, the *Chicago Sun-Times*, and the *Wall Street Journal*.

Ronald A. Pearlman is professor of law at the Georgetown University Law Center. Prior to joining the faculty, he was a tax partner in the law firm of Covington & Burling. Previously, he served in three tax positions with the federal government. In the mid-1960s, Mr. Pearlman served with the Office of Chief Counsel of the Internal Revenue Service in Washington. After fifteen years of private law practice in St. Louis, he returned to Washington in 1983 to serve first as the deputy assistant secretary for tax policy at the U.S. Treasury, and then as the assistant treasury secretary for tax policy, a presidential appointment. At the Treasury, he had overall responsibility for development of the department's 1984 tax reform proposals and President Ronald Reagan's 1985 tax reform recommendations to Congress. He represented the administration during the consideration of the Tax Reform Act of 1986 by the House of Representatives. After a brief return to private practice, he was appointed chief of staff of the Congressional Joint Committee on Taxation, where he served from 1988 to 1990. Over the years, Mr. Pearlman has served in a number of professional organizations and advisory groups, including as vice-chair (government relations) of the American Bar Association Section of Taxation, as a consultant to two tax policy projects of the American Law Institute, and as president of the American Tax Policy Institute. He has also served as a visiting professor at Harvard Law School and on the adjunct faculties of the University of Virginia School of Law and Washington University School of Law in St. Louis. He has lectured at the Japan Ministry of Finance and at the Escuela Superior de Administración y Dirección de Empresas Law School in Barcelona, Spain. Mr. Pearlman has testified before Congress over thirty times on tax policy matters.

Edward C. Prescott is a senior monetary adviser at the Federal Reserve Bank of Minneapolis and is the W. P. Carey Chair of Economics in the W. P. Carey School of Business at Arizona State University. He was awarded the 2004 Nobel Prize in economic sciences for his contributions to dynamic macroeconomics with his work on the time consistency of economic policy and the driving forces behind business cycles. (He shares the prize with Finn Kydland.) Mr. Prescott has held teaching positions at the University of Minnesota, the University of Chicago, Carnegie-Mellon University, and the University of Pennsylvania. He has held a number of visiting professorships at universities throughout the United States and Europe. He has authored more than seventy principal articles in which he addresses topics such as business cycles, economic development, general equilibrium theory, banking and finance, and economic policy. A recent paper explains that Americans work longer hours than Europeans because of the disincentive effect associated with higher taxes in Europe, and shows that these disincentives result in a large loss in well-being for the average European. Another paper develops a methodology for determining whether the stock market is over- or undervalued. Mr. Prescott is currently a fellow of the American Academy of Arts and Sciences and the Econometric Society.

Joel Slemrod is the Paul W. McCracken Collegiate Professor of Business Economics and Public Policy at the Ross School of Business at the University of Michigan, where he also serves as director of the Office of Tax Policy Research. Mr. Slemrod joined the economics department at the

University of Minnesota in 1979. From 1983 to 1984 he was a national fellow at the Hoover Institution, and from 1984 to 1985 he was the senior staff economist for tax policy at the president's Council of Economic Advisers. He has been at Michigan since 1987, and was chairman of the Business Economics Group from 1991 to 1992, and from 1995 to 1998. From 1992 to 1998, Professor Slemrod was editor of the *National Tax Journal*, the leading academic journal devoted to the theory and practice of taxation. Mr. Slemrod has been a consultant to the U.S. Department of the Treasury, the Canadian Department of Finance, the New Zealand Department of Treasury, the World Bank, and the Organisation for Economic Co-operation and Development. He acted as coordinator of the National Bureau of Economic Research project on international taxation. In 1993, Mr. Slemrod was an invited faculty member at the U.S. House Ways and Means Committee Annual Issues Seminar, and he has testified before Congress on domestic and international taxation issues. He is coauthor with Jon Bakija of the recently published book on tax policy titled *Taxing Ourselves: A Citizen's Guide to the Great Debate over Tax Reform* (MIT Press, 1996).

www.ingramcontent.com/pod-product-compliance
Lightning Source LLC
Jackson TN
JSHW011654231224
75956JS00003B/25